THE HARMONIOUS VISION

Studies in Milton's Poetry

THE HARMONIOUS VISION

STUDIES IN MILTON'S POETRY

Enlarged Edition

DON CAMERON ALLEN

THE JOHNS HOPKINS PRESS

BALTIMORE AND LONDON

The Johns Hopkins Press, Baltimore, Maryland 21218
The Johns Hopkins Press Ltd., London

Library of Congress Catalog Card Number 79–117254

ISBN-0-8018-1191-0

Originally published, 1954
Second printing, 1955
Third printing, 1960
Fourth printing, 1963
Enlarged edition, 1970

To Mary

PREFACE TO THE ENLARGED EDITION

EXCEPT FOR a melange of short expository annotations
and the essay on the fifth elegy in *Image and Meaning,* my pub-
lications on Milton's poetry after 1954 have been oblique rather
than direct. When the first version of this book was completed,
I planned a similar study of *Paradise Lost,* and the new concluding chapter, originally contributed to Harris Fletcher's
festschrift, was written to this end. Now I have just about
abandoned the idea of adding another title to the Milton library
unless I could be sure the book would be in Milton's library.
The odds against such an accident are so enormous that I shall
buy no chances; hence, I have brought this stray into the fold.

March, 1970   D. C. A.

PREFACE

IN THE following chapters I have attempted to read some
of Milton's poetry or to comment on some aspects of his genius
in a purely personal way. I do not think that I can insist on
any of my observations as exhausting the total possibilities of
exegesis nor am I sure that my method of approach is sensible
or sensitive. I simply register here what at this date I think
Milton was trying to say, how he said it, and how he succeeded.
I should have been unable to do this unless I had had masters;
hence, I am grateful to Miltonists all over the world and in all
times who have enabled me to form my conclusions. Without
them I could have said nothing.

                                                    D. C. A.
October 25, 1953

CONTENTS

INTRODUCTION

*T*HE Renaissance traded in the market of analogy and one of its most valued illusions can be expressed in a formula: God is a poet and the world his poem; hence the poet is a god and his poetry a new world of his making.[1] From this point of view Milton detaches himself and returns to the more ancient tradition of Hesiod, Homer, and the English Cædmon. The poet is no god, for God himself is, through his intermediaries, the source of all human song. Certain poets, to be sure, may be the analogues of Satan and Belial, for there is poetry enough in Hell; but the proper poet is neither God's simile nor is he capable of creation beyond the fixed order of Nature, the will of God. In fact, the poet and his poems are parts in the essential harmony of creation, and while they are inspired by God, one cannot blaspheme the Deity by likening him to a poet.

There is in *Paradise Lost* a tacit recognition that God, who is the source of proper poetry, is above verse-making. This is why his speeches are " flat," why he speaks like " a school divine." Metaphor and simile are useless to him for he knows what he has created and needs no comparatives. Only once does God slip into a poetic figure (XI. 52–53), and on this occasion we feel that Milton has edited God. The cleavage between God and the poet is clearly brought out in the commentary of Raphael on the Creation week.

We know that the angels are poets, but we also know that in spite of their intelligential being they are almost as limited as mortals in their attempts to praise God and describe his works. Raphael is troubled by his inability to explain heavenly matter to earthly man (V. 564–76) ; and to fulfill his obligation,

[1] See J. C. Scaliger, *Poetices* (1591), 6; Sir Philip Sidney, *The Defence of Poesie* (Cambridge, 1923), 8–9.

he adopts a universal metaphor and relates his message as a symbolic narrative.

> By lik'ning spiritual to corporal forms,
> As may express them best, though what if Earth
> Be but the shadow of Heav'n, and things therein
> Each to other like, more than on earth is thought?

While we read this, we must not forget that God and his mysteries are farther removed from angels than angels are from men; hence, Raphael, though he may understand Heaven's secrets better than Adam, is still forced to talk in poetic comparatives. God can say bluntly: " Let th' Earth / Put forth the verdant Grass, Herb yielding Seed, / And Fruit Tree yielding Fruit after her kind." The Divine fiat then becomes the theme of Raphael's lyric, which, with his long experience in hymnology, he embroiders with poetic ornaments so that Adam with his more restricted comprehension may understand.

> Then Herbs of every leaf, that sudden flow'r'd
> Op'ning thir various colours, and made gay
> Her bosom smelling sweet: and these scarce blown,
> Forth flourish't thick the clust'ring Vine, forth crept
> The smelling Gourd, up stood the corny Reed
> Embattl'd in her field: and the humble Shrub,
> And Bush with frizzl'd hair implicit: last
> Rose as in Dance the stately Trees, and spread
> Thir branches hung with copious Fruit: or gemm'd
> Thir Blossoms (VII. 317–26) .

Though angels may be better poets than men, they are not God's simile. Men are still farther away; hence, Milton cannot think, as Scaliger and Sidney do, that the poet is "another god," but rather does he see poets as inadequate expounders of God's creation. So the poet, since he cannot describe things in essence, is forced to use qualities and degrees. But even here the poet wants final competence because he is himself one of the things. Now Milton knew that all things proclaim the glory of God, but he was also aware that they do this according to their own Godlikeness. Man, and especially the proper poet among men, is best fitted for this task, but the poet's exceptional Godlikeness does not make him like God. At best he is an instrument for the elegant expression of the Divine Will. He becomes, by a figure of rhetoric, both the instrument and the word. " Thou art the Proclamation; and I am / The Trumpet, at whose voyce the people came." With this, the concept of the poet and his duties is wedded to the doctrine of the universal harmony.

The poet's place in the concert of Creation was plain to the Cambridge undergraduate who spoke the second prolusion. The prophet and the poet, Ezekiel and David, are here made one, for we are told by the gifted boy that the philosopher who initiated Pythagoras in the theory of harmony " imitated either the poets or, what is almost the same thing, the divine oracles." He knows, too, that it was Plato who succeeded, according to the book that he will eventually annotate in the lonely tower, in combining the discordant and disharmonious sounds of creation into the great reverberating concord of the *anima mundi.* What is explained in the *Timaeus* by the symbolism of numbers is re-expressed in the *Republic* by myth. The resurrected Greek informs the youthful poet that the ascending souls see the end of the chain of Heaven as a line of light, " that famous golden chain of Jove," as the prolusion puts it, " hanging down from Heaven." The harmonious cosmos of *Paradise Lost* is suspended on this chain, but in the vision of Plato, as in the essay of Milton, it is the spindle of Necessity that hangs therefrom. We know it all from the *Arcades:*

> then listen I
> To the celestial *Sirens'* harmony,
> That sit upon the nine enfolded Spheres
> And sing to those that hold the vital shears
> And turn the Adamantine spindle round,
> On which the fate of gods and men is wound.
> Such sweet compulsion doth in music lie,
> To lull the daughters of *Necessity,*
> And keep unsteady Nature to her law,
> And the low world in measur'd motion draw
> After the heavenly tune, which none can hear
> Of human mould with gross unpurged ear (62–73) .

Pythagoras alone, the prolusion tells us, heard the harmony, and impelled by the music he descended to teach men its basic measures, virtue and wisdom. The sin of Prometheus muted the song, " but if we possessed hearts so pure, so spotless, so snowy, as once upon a time Pythagoras had, then, indeed, would our ears be made to resound and to be completely filled with the most delicious music of the revolving stars; and then all things would return immediately as it were to the golden age." The late Platonic conclusion that men lost the tune of the celestial revolution *ob consortium corporis* is thus adjusted to theology and fastened on the hamartia of Prometheus. A Christian reading that likens Prometheus to Adam, and Pythagoras to Christ, is implied in undertone, but in supplying this silent gloss, Milton is also suggesting that virtue is the way to harmony and that harmony is the center of the vision of the Golden Age. In time he turns this prose into verse and associates in the " Nativity Ode " the ninefold harmony with a fanciful return to the Eden of Adam's first hour. But the revisitation is not done at once.[2]

" At a Solemn Music," " L'Allegro," and " Il Penseroso " are markers on the road back. The former polyphony of the single noted chorus of the universe is best attempted through a union of poetry and music, " Sphere-born harmonious Sisters, Voice and Verse." By them the imagination is expanded to such an elevated vision that it thinks to hear the eternally soaring hymn. Through this marriage of the " *cognatae artes,*" the reason of the hearer is so united with his sensibilities that something like the " prophetic strain " is naturally consequent. The concord of voice and verse begets the sounding vision, and the " undisturbed song of pure concent " prompts the gifted imagination (a ready poet-scholar, thanks to God), so that in its turn, it attempts an echo-like answer. " That we on Earth with undiscording voice / May rightly answer that melodious noise." The transference of music into prophecy demands a vision of per-

[2] I am, of course, indebted to Leo Spitzer, " Classical and Christian Ideas of World Harmony," *Traditio*, II, 409–564; III, 307–64 and Hutton, " Some English Poems in Praise of Music," *English Miscellany*, II, 1–63.

fection similar to that of the Golden Age. To supply this requirement, Milton invents what never was—the music of Eden.

Poets cannot be respectful of history if they wish to remain
poets, so Milton, learned as he is, never scorns the sweet alteration of fact. Neither the Bible nor its expositors hear music in
the Garden, but given his vision through harmony, the poet
fills it with music. What he imagined as a young man, he
annotates in his maturity:

> how often from the steep
> Of echoing Hill or Thicket have we heard
> Celestial voices to the midnight air,
> Sole, or responsive each to other's note
> Singing thir great Creator: oft in bands
> While they keep watch, or nightly rounding walk
> With Heav'nly touch of instrumental sounds
> In full harmonic number join'd, thir songs
> Divide the night, and lift our thoughts to Heaven
>
> (IV. 680–88) .

In Milton's vision there was music before the Fall. Adam first
heard it on the day of his creation, " thou remember'st, for
thou heard'st " (VII. 561) . The music that he hears continually
" above, about, or underneath," he attempts to rephrase in
his Morning Hymn where the full orchestra of creatures is
summoned " to answer the melodious noise." Eve, too, though
on a lesser plane, hears the music and it makes her a poetess.
Her poem is the only love lyric—really the only one that Milton
wrote—in the epic (IV. 641–56) . Her subject, as fitting her
state, is Adam, but it is decorous that she praise God in the
person of her husband.

The Golden Age dies and its music perishes with it. " Dis-
proportioned sin " has jarred against " nature's chime," and
Adam can no longer hear " Cherubic songs by night." His
descendant Jubal will discover a substitute for the lost music
of Heaven (XI. 558–63) and the slow ascent will begin, longer
and more difficult now, towards the threshold of divine harmony. When the hearing has been blessed by the solemn music

of the organ and of the " full voic'd Quire," the eyes also will be hallowed. All Heaven may come before them and the poet, gifted with the strain of prophecy " may see and tell / Of things invisible to mortal sight." The human approximation of the great diapason may father the vision, which itself is a reflection of Heaven, a partial return to the great Sixth Day. This Milton surely believed, but he knew it was only possible to God's elected instrument.

There is a stanza in " The Passion " where the young poet, thinking on Ezekiel, the prophet " by the Vision led," is carried on wings of angels to the towers of Salem. As it comes back into our memory, we think of those maturer statements with which the older poet of *Paradise Lost* explains his divine impulsions.[3] The poet-prophet, not the poet-god, may rediscover the Christian Golden Age when by the hard training of the virtuous way he becomes, through grace, the trumpet of God. The Elder Brother in *Comus* outlines the promise (and Milton variantly describes it in " L'Allegro " and " Il Penseroso ") and its gratifying gain.

> And in clear dream and solemn vision
> Tell her of things that no gross ear can hear,
> Till oft converse with heav'nly habitants
> Begin to cast a beam on th' outward shape,
> The unpolluted temple of the mind,
> And turns it by degrees to the soul's essence,
> Till all be made immortal (457–63) .

Milton knew something of this when he made his second outline for the tragedy of *Paradise Lost* and assigned the prologue to Moses who tells the audience that " they cannot se Adam in the state of innocence by reason of thir sin." This announcement is made more emphatic when we learn that Adam was not to appear in the play until, fallen and miserable, he entered in the fourth act to describe his woes. Sinless vision, in Milton's mind, was the companion of sinless music; and it is, perhaps, significant that only three poet-prophets, Moses on Sinai, Dante

---

[3] I. 6–8, 17–19; IX. 21–24.

on the Purgatorial Mount, and Milton, who ascends as do Michael and the remorseful Adam, " in the Visions of God," have seen at the same time the vision of the Christian Golden Age and heard the perfect harmony of Heaven.[4] But we can follow this thread of song and sight as it makes the warp of the great epic.

Although it enjoys the instruction of many preceding and contending traditions, *Paradise Lost* preserves the visionary qualities that we associate with the utterances of the prophets. The poem begins with a remembrancer of those hallowed loci of prophetic experience, Horeb, Sinai, Mount Zion, Siloam; and, as at the end Adam prompted by Michael will look into the future, so in the opening lines Milton led by the Heavenly Muse—" for Heav'n hides nothing from thy view / Nor the deep Tract of Hell "—peers into the past. We have hardly begun to read the epic before we are aware of this distinction and reminded of familiar phrases: " the hand of the Lord was upon me " or " the word of Jehovah came unto me." The sense of vision that touches us as we begin to read is constantly renewed as we move up and down in the wide territories of a universe fresh in time. We hear a voice crying, " Woe to the inhabitants of the earth," and we know that it is John of Patmos, whose angel we see standing in the sun. These moments of prophetic recognition are frequent, but we are also made aware of the tissue of vision by a process of absolute dimension.

In " L'Allegro " there is a set distance between the poet and the common experience that he describes, but the poet's aloofness does not shut the reader out of the scene. He may watch the morrice or listen to the shepherds " chatting in a rustic row "; he may also join the dance, if he wishes, and tell his legends of Queen Mab. The same is not true of *Paradise Lost*. The poet's distance is always the reader's distance—we look from afar or it is all related to us at second hand. We play Adam to Milton's Michael. We look down on Eden; we

[4] Dante, *Purg.*, XXIX. 22–30; see J. H. Hanford, " That Shepherd, Who First Taught the Chosen Seed," *University of Toronto Quarterly*, VIII, 403–19.

see Hell from away. The war in Heaven, the consult in Hell, the voyage of Satan, the temptation and fall, the councils in Heaven, and the final remorse and regret are seen by us through the small end of our glasses. When we read the *Iliad*, we have the feeling that we are present at the quarrel between Achilles and Agamemnon, that we know Thersites, bandy-legged, lame of foot, slope-shouldered, and warped-of-head. We sit at Dido's feast with Aeneas and we are armed on the field when Camilla dies. But though we have a more personal interest in the Fall of Man, we see it darkly because the text that lies before us is really the harmonious vision of a vision.

If for the poet and his readers, the poem has the quality of a vision, it has a similar quality for the giant characters who people it. For Satan and his peers, the harmonious vision is lost, and there is no miracle that will restore it—only the beguiling miracle of an easy temptation which seals the doom of the tempter. The doom is decreed on the day that Christ is named vice-regent of Heaven:

> him who disobeys
> Mee disobeys, breaks union, and that day
> Cast out from God and blessed vision, falls
> Into utter darkness (V. 611–14) .

For Mammon, this second punishment of the damned is probably not too severe, for he admired the golden pavements more " Then aught divine or holy else enjoy'd / In vision beatific " (I. 683–84) . Others do not escape so lightly. For Satan, the decadent poet, and for the " mild " demons who " sing / With notes Angelical to many a Harp " (II. 547–48) , this is a sharp punishment made keener when, after the temptation, their proposed songs of praise become in serpent throats the antithesis of music and poetry and their eyes are deceived by the dusty vision of an orchard fair but false. Then Hell, itself, devoid of the harmonious vision becomes the symbol of the privation of harmony as, by inversion, the harmonious vision is the symbol of the annihilation of Hell.

For if such holy Song
Enwrap our fancy long,
Time will run back, and fetch the age of gold . . .

And Hell itself will pass away,
And leave her dolorous mansions to the peering day.

The equation of the harmonious vision, so perfect in Heaven, so void in Hell, so near to him who has the " prophetic strain," so far from the despairing sinner, is repeated on different tones in the biographies of Adam and Eve. It is ironical, perhaps, that Adam, who is so learned in psychology that he ventures to diagnose Eve's dream only to reveal his ignorance of the nature of satanic illusion, is unaware that both he and Eve live in a vision. The first eight books of *Paradise Lost* are a commentary on a vision of a world in which evil is still unknown save as an abstraction. The vision vanishes significantly enough when the eyes of the first parents are opened and they know their sinfulness. With this curious awakening the music ends, the vision passes, and they are neither poets nor prophets again. This growing to comprehension is symbolically indicated by the troublesome dreams that harass the lecherous pair before their ultimate arousing, " with conscious dreams / Encumber'd " (IX. 1050–51). With these lesser dreams the great vision closes and Adam can no longer imagine that they are secure from evil and permanent in creation.

There are earlier and God-given dreams within the great vision, and the first of them is, strangely enough, a dream within a vision. Shortly after his creation, Adam is taken by a " soft oppression " so that for one vivid moment he thinks he is returning to a state of nothingness. He is conveyed to a garden and finds himself in a field of savoury fruit. " Whereat I wak'd, and found / Before mine Eyes all real " (VIII. 309–10). But this is not the last dream that he has in the vision; once again " Mine eyes he clos'd, but op'n left the Cell / Of Fancy my internal sight " (460–61). He awakes to find it truth, for the companion whom he desired is with him. In an obvious way, these are all dreams in what is later called the " Visions of

God "; they are true dreams, too, for they are attended by the
great vision of the flowery garden planted eastward in Eden
and by the poetic miracle of Eve. Eve's dream is unlike Adam's
because it is outside the vision itself; it is true but not the truth.
It predicts the end of truth, of the great vision.

The great vision ends, but another vision is provided by
God through his instrument, the poet-prophet. In this, the
ways of God are justified to men; and to prove his unquestioned
assertion of Providence, Milton invents the vision of consolation
as he had invented the music of the Christian Golden Age.
There is no theological ground for the last two books of the
epic; the author of Genesis sends the fallen pair out of the
garden under an enigmatic curse. The poet-prophet, looking
backward and forward in time, cannot permit the harmonious
vision to fade without some hint of the greater vision of redemption. God, through the ministry of the paraclete, supplied
Milton with the facts and Milton provided the poetic exegesis
for the essential text: "ipsa conteret caput tuum, et tu insidi-
aberis calcaneo eius."

It is Adam who has the first vision after the one in which
he had lived vanishes; yet Eve, who has had, as far as we know,
only dreams of satanic origin and those bred by the after-sleep
of lechery, is not thrust out from the place of her beloved
flowers without a consolatory dream. "Go, waken Eve," says
Michael,

> Her also I with gentle Dreams have calm'd
> Portending good, and all her spirits compos'd
> To meek submission (XII. 594–97).

In comfort she awakes: "by mee the Promis'd Seed shall all
restore." Eve, as her husband, has something of the "prophetic
strain." The harmonious vision is lost but it can be won again.
Towards its recapture, Milton, true son of Eve, expended the
full powers of his poetic life.

THE HARMONIOUS VISION
Studies in Milton's Poetry

I

THE SEARCH FOR THE PROPHETIC STRAIN:

"L'Allegro" and "Il Penseroso"

*I*T should not pass unnoticed that there is a concealed unity in *The Shepheardes Calender* established by the confused meditations of the new poet who is attempting to plot the maze of life before he treads it. Snared by the tradition and by a sensibility of purpose, he inquires of himself the way. Is it love, or art, or religion? This is no easy question for him to answer because the intricacy of paths cross and recross, hindering immensely the prospect of direction. The troubadours, whose descendant Spenser was, had found the road through the grace of sophistry and the merit of compromise; but in 1580, the troubadour was only a chivalric memory, and the question, answered finally in the *Hymnes* and the *Amoretti*, was again an open one.

A half century later, Milton had a far easier choice. He had tuned his harp in Sion and not in Toulouse; hence one of the ways, the sweet and gallant course of love, was not for his walking. He had his Dantesque hour on that spring day, memorialized in the seventh elegy, when he saw the girl who surpassed in loveliness all her companions. She vanished and was never seen again. "Interea misero quae iam mihi sola placebat / Ablata est, oculis non reditura meis." The incident is familiar, but the eventuation is not. She becomes no vaporous embodiment of an ideal, a Beatrice, a Rosalind. She is not only erased from the book of memory, but she and her kind will shortly become like Amaryllis with whom one *sports* or like Neaera who traps her lovers in the uncouth *tangles* of her hair.

3

For Milton, dedicated to other services, romantic love cannot be even the literary artifice that it was for some of his loveless contemporaries.

The choice of ways was made still simpler for Milton because he early decided to combine the other two courses; so the paths of dissent became for him a kingsway of agreement. When I write this I know that I am begging for disapproval, since it has become customary to observe that Milton, though theologically learned, was deficient in religious feeling. Southwell, Herbert, Crashaw, I am told, knew God, whereas Milton attempted only to explain him. A series of critics have informed me that he was majorly a theological poet who festooned the abstract concepts of divinity with the metallic metaphors of a Latinized style. Of the inward fierceness that is generated by overwhelming religious experience he had nothing. Such is the conclusion of those who think of religion as a kind of emotional experience similar in its appetite to swooning at a melodrama or drooling over an inhaler of Napoleon brandy. Milton, even as a young man, knew better than this; he knew that God thought eternally without the obstruction of emotional shivers. This was his image of the deity and in this image he chose to dwell, to shape thereby the route that would best lead him to this end. The nature of this route is partly revealed in " L'Allegro " and " Il Penseroso," and they must be read, not as two poems, but rather as a single utterance on an exalted proposal.

Johnson unbent enough to describe these poems as " noble efforts of the imagination "; and though he thought of them as representing the character and activities of the " chearful " and the pensive man, he noticed that both men were lonely. " Both Mirth and Melancholy are solitary, silent inhabitants of the breast that neither receive nor transmit communications; no mention is therefore made of a philosophical friend or a pleasant companion." Johnson is right; the poet is as lonely as God and to some extent he shares in God's stasis. He may walk " not unseen " in " L'Allegro " and " unseen " in " Il Penseroso " but there is practically no other motion in him. The poems were written in a room and to a large degree they remain in a room, although imaginatively they seem to be out-of-doors. They are permeated by a sense of wall; they have an aloofness and a detachment from the wider dimensions of the world that is symbolically described in them and from the vigorous activities of the men who people this world. There is tribulation enough in the web of the verse, but it is of an intellectual sort and it is characterized by the occasional syntactical confusions that trouble the reader as the poet himself was troubled. In spite of this, there broods over the poems a dominating stillness as if the poet were already at the state of satisfaction that the concluding lines of the second poem predict.

Although these are the poems of a solitary man, they anticipate an even greater quest for creative solitude. " L'Allegro " begins in a morning room where the windows are blinded by vines; " Il Penseroso " ends in a church as the light of the rising sun is muted by painted glass, " casting a dim religious light." The final expectation of the meditating poet is the supreme privacy of the hermit's " mossy cell." We pass from room to room through the twilight of the human imagination, " As when the Sun new ris'n / Looks through the Horizontal misty Air / Shorn of his Beams." Broad day pours its light through only the first forty lines of " L'Allegro," but even here it is obscured by clouds, by smoke, and by " the Chequer'd shade." " Hide me from Day's garish eye," cries the poet as dawn begins to sift through the leaves in " Il Penseroso," where the moon at her zenith measures out her light " through a fleecy cloud." The colors of both poems are grays, browns, subdued blues, lighted blacks, and, almost as we watch, we see them veil the ephemeral numerals of the finite world clock. From lark to nightingale, from dawn to nightset, the shadow moves circularly on the dial, tracing the procession of common experience. These temporal episodes have been variously admired as constituting the essence of the poem; yet they are mainly clichés of only ancillary importance. They have a total symbolic value, but in their separateness they are simply an alphabet of common experience easily recited by anyone.

Milton certainly knew that he was not the first poet to select affective episodes to expound the turning of the earth. Many of his poetic counters, as the annotators have found, had been used before. The lark, the cock, the nightingale, the bee, the cricket had long been loud as sentinels of the day or as nocturnal musicians. The monody of living waters is a traditional accomplice of Sleep and Dreams. The plowman, the mower, the milkmaid, the shepherd had formerly followed their trades not only in literary but in artistic accounts of the hours, the months, the year. These *impresas* are so constantly representative of the imagery of day and night that a contemporary of Milton's would have acknowledged them at once and added many others.

Milton himself used some of them in the first prolusion and he knew of others: the capering she-goat, the marigold, the rose—creatures of day; then those pejorative symbols of the evil aspect of night: thieves, murderers, goblins, ghosts, owls, and hags. Interesting as they are, these reiterated devices are not the main source of the poems' virtue. They are some of the instruments in the orchestra, but in themselves they are not the music which is produced by their ascending confluence. According to the rules of epic variety they will be used later for the descriptions of day and night in the fourth and fifth books of *Paradise Lost*. Then they will be refined and implicative to the degree that they will have a more intimating and a more organic containment. They will in this final appearance not seem so unattached, so capable of desultory rearrangement as they do in this first performance to him who reads them out of the pattern; in fact, they will gain in poetic intensity in the epic because this apparent earlier separateness will seem to be erased. Yet this illusive separateness is produced not so much from lack of literary skill as from the agony of a creative struggle. To say this is to negate all of my previous remarks about the solitary quietness which is the first impression that I abstract from the poems, but the negation is not real because this impression of struggle provides me with a synthetic antithesis that permits me to discern a new basic tone.

The nonhortatory section of " L'Allegro " begins with the song of the lark and the crowing of the cock; that of " Il Penseroso " with a poetic essay on the nightingale. In Milton's age the three birds were symbols of vigilance. The summoner lark was the emblem of the daily resurrection of the world. The cock that brought the sun up and that marked the hours of the night with his crowing was the symbol of watchfulness and for this reason was reproduced in effigy on spires. The nightingale was alleged in the books of the ornithologists to be sleepless. The notion of the alert man seems to me to be stronger in these poems than that of the cheerful or the pensive man; it is the other side of the quiet solitary and it is the necessary component of the subsurface struggle. The vigilance indicated is not one of open activity; it is not a matter of constant gesture or violent flourishes. The poet is always awake, but this awakeness is disguised by the divine stillness of thought. His mind does the body's labor. There is in neither poem a place for sleep. The poet of " Il Penseroso " seeks repose after daybreak, but the poet of " L'Allegro " rises with the sun. The slumber that is sought is not real sleep; it is a poetic sleep filled with " strange mysterious dreams." This is an important point in the total exegesis of the poems and I shall return to it. For the moment it can be observed that as " wanton heed " and " giddy cunning " qualify the musical pleasures of " L'Allegro," so, perhaps, " alert quiet " is a tone that possesses both poems.

With this statement, if it has not been apparent before, I join the party of those who see these poems as deeply serious and take issue with the theses of Tillyard [1] and to some extent with those of Brooks.[2] I am ready to agree that the first prolusion contains the seeds of the poems and I am ready to assume that the poems came to flower in *Paradise Lost*, but I cannot think of the poems as metrical annexes to the prolusion from which they are so different in purpose. The prolusion has the " social tone " that Tillyard and Brooks find in the poems. I look for this tone in vain, and I expect that they have unwit-

[1] *The Miltonic Setting* (New York, 1949), 1–28.
[2] *The Well Wrought Urn* (New York, 1947), 47–61.

tingly transferred it from the prose. In "L'Allegro," which must be the most social poem of the two, there is nothing so familiar as the "*academici*," or "*pace vestra*," or "*causam dignemini meam vestris ornare suffragiis*," or the many other suggestions of the second person plural that we hear in the prolusion. The plowman may be "near at hand," but he is so intent on his plowing and his whistling that he does not salute the poet nor the poet him. We are not sure that the beauty really lives in the castle; certainly, if she does, she is unknown to the stranger poet. The stock Arcadian characters are observed from a safe distance or overheard at their chatter while the poet takes his ease at a rural inn. He does not join in the haying, the dancing, or the tale-telling. In the city he is also a spectator if the things that he witnesses there are real at all; this I can say because Milton tells me that the events described are such "as youthful poets dream." He attends the theater; he listens to concerts. His interest in men and their daily affairs is passive, almost disinterested.

Either I or the poems are devoid of humor, for I cannot read them as *jeux d'esprit* or burlesques. The hortatory beginnings are bombastic, but they are no more bombastic than public prayer. In "L'Allegro," after the worst sort of melancholy is dismissed, Euphrosyne, chief of the graces, is invited to attend the poet because as a mythologist Milton knew that she was the companion of the Horae. He rectifies her ancestry, making her, in the Baconian fashion, a kind of nature myth and as such more readily accessible to men. With her he associates the oread Liberty, the "Mountain Nymph." The qualification suggests political liberty, but I agree with Brooks that Milton intends the sylvan lady to stand for something larger than this though I cannot share Brooks' special materialistic interpretation. To any man of the seventeenth century *liberty* meant what *libertas* meant to an ancient: *manumission*. What has enslaved the poet, we must ask, and from what does he desire to be freed? "Hence loathed Melancholy / Of Cerberus and blackest midnight born." The poems contain the traces of a struggle, but they also describe a progress from an enslaving dissatisfaction to an ultimate gratification. The original distemper is implied in the lines subsequent to the invocation of " L'Allegro."

> Then to come *in spite of sorrow*,
> And at my window bid good morrow.

Why is the poet (for it is the poet and certainly not the lark) sad at the commencement of his progress, at the outset of the struggle? I cannot pretend to know, but a juxtaposition of images in the center of the poem may be important.

Having rapidly presented the reader with a stereotyped catalogue of dawn events, Milton writes,

> Mountains on whose barren breast
> The labouring clouds do often rest.

At first reading, these lines seem hardly worthy of Wordsworth; yet they conceal, perhaps, a useful indication. The fertile clouds about to give birth to rain and free themselves of their burden writhe in agony on the summits of the sterile mountains. " Barren breast " is a figure not unlike " wanton heed," and " labouring . . . rest " is similar to the tonal " alert quiet." The calendar of Milton's writing would suggest that artistic sterility and the struggle for expressive birth were not far from his mind. The dismissals of the unfruitful melancholy and the infertile folly join in making firm this presumption. The poems were, I expect, begotten of a struggle; they partially tell the history of this struggle; and they outline the process that will lead to the eventual fecundation of the poet's imagination. But to return to Tillyard's theses.

There is no doubt that the opening passages of " Il Penseroso " are less boisterous than those of " L'Allegro," and though the metrical cursus is similar, Tillyard is tacitly ready to exempt the invocation of the former poem from censure. The difference between the two passages is teasing because it may mark a growth of confidence. The first part of " L'Allegro " obtains much of its loudness from a liberal use of dental and palatal spirants; the voiceless labial spirant that controls the second hortation supplies a note of deliberation that is emphasized by the delaying quality of the voiced labial stop. The *mora* in the second invocation is further enhanced by the fact that the meaning is not immediately clear. It would probably be somewhat unintelligible to those readers who have no knowledge of the tropes of Renaissance psychology. What Milton says in the first poem's invocation is at once obvious: Melancholy born of Midnight in a dark and horrid place is exiled to a desert cave. In the invocation to the second poem, he banishes the ungoverned imagination, setting aside delusions fostered by irrational thought. The mode of the first invocation is rejection; that of the second, though rejection is there, perpends the grave theme of the poem.

The second invocation is more accomplished and so is the poem that it introduces. In " L'Allegro " there is an abrupt division between the invitation and the main body of the poem. This is not true of " Il Penseroso." " To hear the lark " comes as a separate verse paragraph after the variation on the Elizabethan " come-live-with-me-and-be-my-love " motif. The transition in " Il Penseroso " between the invitation to Contemplation and Silence and the phrase " 'Less Philomel will deign a song " is more fluid and skillful. The poetic components of " Il Penseroso " seem to glide out of each other by brilliant acts of association. Pursuing the moon, the poet, like Endimion, finds himself climbing towards her on a hillside. From this point he more readily hears the notes of the curfew as they are carried by the stream of air. But the air is uncongenial so he retires to his fire and seated before it hears the snugger voices of the cricket and the bellman. One phrase naturally follows another; they are not appliqued to the piece as they are in " L'Allegro."

I have said that these poems have little social quality, that the poet lives to himself. It is for this reason that " Il Penseroso " gains in power; it is much more solitary and, hence, a more personal poem. Although Milton had previously declaimed against Night in the prolusion, his experiences of night as he relates them in the second poem were certainly more keenly felt than the experiences recounted in " L'Allegro."

Books read are part of this autobiography but only the most obvious part. " *Cynthia* checks her Dragon yoke, / Gently o'er th' accustom'd Oak." The oak is real, and when Milton wrote that passage, he remembered it in all its nocturnal convolutions. The same may be said of the minutiae of the morning shower:

> usher'd with a shower still,
> When the gust hath blown his fill,
> Ending on the rustling Leaves,
> With minute drops from off the Eaves.

These lines have in them a conviction of observation that is quite beyond that of the traditional descriptions of the first poem. A similar conviction evolves from the particularity of the momentary dream in the " close covert by some Brook." This is " the bee loud glade," but Milton was there first. The commentators who have tiresomely uncovered analogues for many passages of " L'Allegro " are halted by these figures, for they are not borrowed but are rather the slow distillations of the poet's life.

The differences between these two poems lead me to suppose that " Il Penseroso " is a more mature poem than " L'Allegro," and though I cannot think of either poem as written as an appendix to the prolusion—as the prolusion seems to have been spoken as an appendix to a college play—yet I am ready to suppose that " L'Allegro " is a somewhat younger effort. I want to read these poems together, to hear them as the poet's plans for himself outlined in a series of rising steps; and so it is with reluctance that I think of them, if not poetically separate, as at least temporally apart. " L'Allegro " may have been written during the last years at Cambridge; it may have sprung directly from the prolusion though its purpose was not, I hope, to make the men of Christ's grin. " Il Penseroso " is the poem of a poet who has found his way. It magnifies some of the insights of " L'Allegro," but it is the work of a man who is almost free from the sterile melancholy that once invested him. In the second poem, Milton is not only purged of his black bile but of his academic obligations; he is cultivating his " trim

Gardens " in the " retired leasure " that is proper to his temperament.

To the detriment of the close study of these poems is the trite notion that all that is in them is on the surface, a judgment invariably made on the poetry of young men. Generations, we are told, have taken pleasure in these poems because they have none of the vexing subtilities that obscure Milton's other works. The repetition of this absurdity has disguised the fact that a more sensitive meaning resides in the matter of these poems than has usually been noticed. Yet Milton implies and sometimes openly states that in these poems " more is meant than meets the ear." One of these implications is found in the lines on Chaucer.

> Or call up him that left half told
> The story of *Cambuscan* bold,
> Of *Camball* and of *Algarsife*,
> And who had *Canace* to wife,
> That own'd the virtuous Ring and Glass,
> And of the wond'rous Horse of Brass,
> On which the *Tartar* King did ride.

Here we ask, as we do in the case of Spenser, why this tale of all the *Canterbury Tales* caught the fancy of the poet? There is, of course, something captivating about a fragmentary narrative, but the squire had more than his share of long-windedness and had Chaucer permitted him to finish his story, he might have been telling it yet. I expect that Milton was not so interested in the tale as in the symbolic emphases: the ring, the glass, the brass horse, not the magic sword. The horse conquered space; the mirror made known the secrets of men; and the ring, those of nature. Spenser was charmed with the theme of courtesy and with a court similar to Gloriana's; Milton was enchanted by the symbols of intellectual power. There is a connection that is probably not entirely fortuitous between Chaucer's

> Ther is no foul that fleeth under the hevene
> That she ne shal wel understonde his stevene,

> And knowe his mening openly and pleyn,
> And answere him in his langage ageyn
> And every gras that groweth up-on rote
> She shal eek knowe, and whom it wol do bote   (149–54).

and Milton's

> Where I may sit and rightly spell
> Of every Star that Heav'n doth shew,
> And every Herb that sips the dew.

We do not know how the seventeenth century read Chaucer, but I think that we can assume that Milton saw in this tale a symbolic narrative and that this perception had something to do with the effluence of his two poems.

But this passage does not stand alone in its suggestiveness; another may be fittingly adduced:

> Where I may oft out-watch the *Bear*,
> With thrice great *Hermes*, . . .

The mechanics of Ursa Major have been elucidated by the commentators who inform us that it never sets. Milton, however, out-distances his editors for he directs us to the Ποιμάνδρης where we learn that this constellation is a symbol of perfection, of a never declining motion that makes an exact circle around Polaris. "The Bear who revolves upon herself, and carries round with her the whole Kosmos." [3] But how may this concept of perfection be realized? "Thrice great *Hermes*" joins with the "spirit of Plato" to instruct us. The Ποιμάνδρης written by the eldest philosopher, as Milton thought of him, flows into the *Timaeus* written by the best. Plato's achievement of the realm of essences is well known; Hermes' advice has a Christian condition that must have entranced the young poet. "The immortal mind that hath forsook / Her mansion in this fleshly nook," writes Hermes, proceeds upward and discards some of its material tatters at each of the spheres.

[3] *Op. cit.*, V. 4.

And thereupon, having been stripped of all that was wrought upon him by the structure of the heavens, he ascends to the substance of the eighth sphere, being now possessed of his own proper power; and he sings, together with those who dwell there, hymning the Father; and they that are there rejoice with him at his coming. And being made like to those with whom he dwells, he hears the Powers, who are above the substance of the eighth sphere, singing praise to God with a voice that is theirs alone. And thereafter, each in his turn, they mount upward to the Father; they give themselves up to the Powers, and becoming Powers themselves, they enter into God.[4]

The mind purified of its mundane excrescences becomes the music of God. The earthly expression of this experience,

> There let the pealing Organ blow
> To the full voic'd Quire below,
> In Service high and Anthems clear,
> As may with sweetness, through mine ear,
> Dissolve me into extasies,
> And bring all Heav'n before mine eyes,

becomes in its ultimate experience a knowable reality.

This knowable reality is not attained through an excess of religious emotions or through the exercises of the mystic, but through universal knowledge as a prelude to universal thought. Hermes displays the chart of necessary experiences.

Leap clear of all that is corporeal, and make yourself grow to a like expanse with that greatness which is beyond all measure; rise above all time, and become eternal; then you will apprehend God. Think that for you too nothing is impossible; deem that you too are immortal, and that you are able to grasp all things in your thought, to know every craft and every science; find your home in the haunts of every living creature; make yourself higher than all heights, and lower than all depths; bring together in yourself all opposites of quality, heat and cold, dryness and fluidity; think that you are everywhere at once, on land, at sea, in heaven; think that you

---

4 *Ibid.*, I. 25–26.

are not yet begotten, that you are in the womb, that you are young, that you are old, that you have died, that you are in the world beyond the grave; grasp in your thought all this at once, all times and places, all substances and qualities and magnitudes together; then you can apprehend God.[5]

By this intellectual effort those who have *gnosis* will know God. It is the culminating point of Hermes' philosophy. Though the end is different in that it predicts a preparation for an experience rather than the experience itself, the particularized proposal of the Cambridge student who wrote the third prolusion is similar in intent.

How much better it would be, fellow students, and how much more worthy of your name, to make at this time a tour as it were with your eyes about the whole earth as represented on the map and view the places trodden by ancient heroes, and to travel through the regions made famous by wars, by triumphs, and even by the tales of illustrious poets: now to cross the raging Adriatic, now to approach unharmed flame-capped Aetna; then to observe the customs of men and the governments of nations, so admirably arranged; thence to investigate and to observe, the natures of all living creatures; from these to plunge the mind into the secret powers of stones and plants. Do not hesitate, my hearers, to fly even up to the skies, there to behold those multiform aspects of the clouds, the massy power of the snow, and the source of those tears of early morn; next to peer into the caskets of the hail and to survey the arsenals of the thunderbolts. Nor let what Jupiter or Nature veils from you be concealed when a baleful and enormous comet ofttimes threatens a conflagration from heaven; nor let the most minute little stars be hidden from you, however many there may be scattered and straying between the two poles. Yea, follow as companion the wandering sun, and subject time itself to a reckoning and demand the order of its everlasting journey. Nay, let not your mind suffer itself to be hemmed in and bounded by the same limits as the earth, but let it wander also outside the boundaries of the world. Finally, what is after all the most important matter,

[5] *Ibid.*, XI. 20b.

let it learn thoroughly to know itself and at the same time those holy minds and intelligences, with whom hereafter it will enter into everlasting companionship.[6]

The talented youth has some of the professional philosopher's abstract boldness and his procedure has a certain likeness to that of the hermetic thinker. This procedure explains the total structure of the two poems.

About the time that Milton was summarizing his method in prose, he made a verse attempt that adumbrates the process of " L'Allegro " and " Il Penseroso "

> Yet I had rather, if I were to choose,
> Thy service in some graver subject use,
> Such as may make thee search thy coffers round,
> Before thou clothe my fancy in fit sound:
> Such where the deep transported mind may soar
> Above the wheeling poles, and at Heav'n's door
> Look in, and see each blissful Deity
> How he before the thunderous throne doth lie,
> Listening to what unshorn *Apollo* sings
> To th' touch of golden wires, while *Hebe* brings
> Immortal Nectar to her Kingly Sire:
> Then passing through the Spheres of watchful fire,
> And misty Regions of wide air next under,
> And hills of Snow and lofts of piled Thunder,
> May tell at length how green-ey'd *Neptune* raves,
> In Heav'n's defiance mustering all his waves;
> Then sing of secret things that came to pass
> When Beldam Nature in her cradle was;
> And last of Kings and Queens and *Heroes* old,
> Such as the wise *Demodocus* once told
> In solemn Songs at King *Alcinous'* feast,
> While sad *Ulysses'* soul and all the rest
> Are held with his melodious harmony
> In willing chains and sweet captivity (29–52) .

The movement in these lines from " Hail native Language " is downward and the tone is pagan; in the later poems the total

6 *Works* (New York, 1936) , XII, 169–71.

direction is reversed. The structure of " L'Allegro " and " Il Penseroso " is based on a daily but continued ascent. The revolution of the earth presents at each degree of its rotation a new gradation by which the poet rises towards a comprehension of his created end, towards the " everlasting companionship " with " holy minds and intelligences." " L'Allegro " describes the lower level of each degree; " Il Penseroso " the higher. By a continued mounting of the slopes of the intellect from common experience, to intellectual experience, to religious inspiration, the poet trusts to arrive at the supreme poetic gratification.

> Till old experience do attain
> To somthing like Prophetic strain.

For this reason, the dynamic symbol of the poem is the tower, solitariness and loneliness in itself, but truly much more than that.

Above the horizon of " L'Allegro " stand "Towers and Battlements " and " Tow'red Cities " directing our attention to the " high lonely Tow'r " of " Il Penseroso." This is the most important tower because it has no existence outside the mind of the poet. It is, in fact, his mind and in its immateriality it is similar to the " watch-tow'r " that stands above the early lines of " L'Allegro." Both towers have a supraphysical reality and for that reason they cast long shadows on the flatter physical aspects of the poems. There is, of course, a literal interpretation of the " lonely tower " which the Renaissance would quickly comprehend. Luther wrote in a tower; Don Quixote read his Palmerin and his Amadis in a high room over his courtyard; Montaigne, having returned home to recline on the bosoms of the learned virgins, lived in a tower. Milton's tower is different; it is at once a refuge and a beacon. It may be explicated anagogically.

As the midnight lamp shone down on the pages of the *Timaeus*, it lighted the passage, I imagine, where the mind of man is compared to a tower, an ἀκρόπολις, from which orders dictated by the reason were dispatched to the body (70a). The critical gloss on this passage would have referred the reader to the *Republic*, where the mind is said to be the watch-tower of the soul τῆς ψυχῆς ἀκρόπολιν (560b). Other Greeks seized on this analogy and by transcription it became the *arx* of the Latins. Pliny uses it so [7] and Cicero proclaims the mind the mirific tower of the body.[8] It is one of those self-propagating images and, collated with Hebraic usages, it penetrated the writings of the Christian Church and found a place in English poetry. Spenser knows this tower and makes it the citadel of Alma's house; Donne urges his readers to ascend to the "watch-towre." [9] It congregates with the admonition of Isaiah, "*contemplare in specula*" and with the response: "My lord, I stand continually upon the watchtower in the daytime, and I am set in my ward whole nights." [10] The earthly tower is equated with alertness, with continued intellectual and devotional occupation. The poet must inhabit the tower so that he can find the cell. Here, attended by the "Cherub Contemplation" he must examine his "old experience" until he has transformed it into the "prophetic strain." Common experience is the way to the tower; intellectual experience is the tower; total experience is the substance of the poems.

The structure of the poems rests on the rising stairs of the tower. It is the symbol of the poet's program of artistic progress, though for the moment it is only confusedly envisioned. The mature Milton will return to this notion again in his account of the once possible evolution of man towards the angelic state,[11] but at that time he will know that it is a concept incapable of realization, a betraying myth, yet then he will also have acquired the gratification that these poems postulate. But when he wrote these poems the gratification was not yet his, and the agony of their composition comes from the fact that though he could see the end as through a mist, he was not sure of his direction. As he writes, the way becomes brighter and finally he can plot the total distance.

[7] *Hist. Nat.*, XI. 134.
[8] *De Nat. Deor.*, II. 140.
[9] "The Second Anniversary," 290–300.
[10] XXI. 5, 8.
[11] *Paradise Lost*, V. 469–503.

The first milestone in the course is measured by the common experiences recorded in " L'Allegro ": the plowman, the milkmaid, the mower, the shepherd, the rustic scene, tourneys of arms and wit, the festival of marriage, the theater, the orchestra. All of these experiences are escorted by secular music that is lacking in polyphony: the song of the lark, the crowing of the cock, the whistling of the plowman, the singing of the milkmaid, the hum of the whetstone on the scythe, the music of the bells and the rebeck, the melic softness of Lydian airs. The eventual union of verse and music is the guidepost to " Il Penseroso " where common experience fades away but the music continues. The uninterrupted flow of harmonious sound between the two poems is personified and differentiated by the sundered emphases on the Orphic legend. In " L'Allegro " Orpheus hears the music; it is given to him from " the hidden soul of harmony." In " Il Penseroso " the embodied soul of Orpheus makes the music that forces " Hell grant what Love did seek." The natural poetry of the first phrasing is passive; it comes without struggle. In the second stage, the poet, called into a new life, reproduces the song in a kind of second creation.

The second milestone is the tower. Common experience is shut out and secular music is subdued because the experience here is of the mind and particular. Alone, separated from the enticements of sensation, the poet finds in the writings of those who have reached the final gratification the necessary invigorating intellectual experience. This is a higher experience than that of " L'Allegro " but the first experience promotes the second; it is the rise of the step but not the tread. The difference and the similarity between the two may be translated by the dreams of " L'Allegro " and " Il Penseroso." The poet of " L'Allegro " dreams " on Summer eves by haunted streams " of the purely secular: pomp, feast, revelry, masks, antique pageantry, the matter of common experience. The poet of " Il Penseroso " has a " strange mysterious dream " not easily glossed by the ordinary experience of men. The dream is one of the steps in the progress, but the substance of the dream, though in both instances it is associated with watery sounds, is different. That of " L'Allegro " is on a slightly inferior level to that of

" Il Penseroso," yet it constitutes the rise of the step. The total process is contained in the last thirty lines of the second poem, " where more is meant than meets the ear." To make a closer reading possible, I reprint the lines.

> There in close covert by some Brook,
> Where no profaner eye may look,
> Hide me from Day's garish eye,
> While the Bee with Honied thigh,
> That at her flow'ry work doth sing,
> And the Waters murmuring
> With such consort as they keep,
> Entice the dewy-feather'd Sleep;
> And let some strange mysterious dream
> Wave at his Wings in Airy. stream,
> Of lively portraiture display'd,
> Softly on my eye-lids laid.
> And as I wake, sweet music breathe
> Above, about, or underneath,
> Sent by some spirit to mortals good,
> Or th'unseen Genius of the Wood.
> But let my due feet never fail
> To walk the studious Cloister's pale,
> And love the high embowed Roof,
> With antic Pillars massy proof,
> And storied Windows richly dight,
> Casting a dim religious light.
> There let the pealing Organ blow
> To the full voic'd Quire below,
> In Service high and Anthems clear,
> As may with sweetness, through mine ear,
> Dissolve me into extasies,
> And bring all Heav'n before mine eyes.
> And may at last my weary age
> Find out the peaceful hermitage,
> The Hairy Gown and Mossy Cell,
> Where I may sit and rightly spell
> Of every Star that Heav'n doth shew,
> And every Herb that sips the dew;
> Till old experience do attain
> To somthing like Prophetic strain.

These lines give the immediate effect of a rhapsodic epitome of ascending passion repeated on two sensory tones and proclaiming the ultimate gratification, the end of the poet's progress, now glimpsed but as yet not consummated. There is a ritualistic solemnity about the opening phrases: " Where no profaner eye may look." A mystery is about to take place and the uninitiated are dismissed. This aura of mystery is magnified when we remember that St. Melancholia's face was too bright " to hit the Sense of human sight " and that, as a consequence, it was covered with a dark veil, much as the face of a god is hidden when he shows himself to men. The mystery is further amplified by the two sensory tones of sight and sound, constantly invoked throughout the two poems, and the superior ministers of this whole passage. *Eye* and *ear* are the reiterated words. But there is a difference between the sensations of sight and sound in these closing verses and this difference is made stout by a purple line of demarcation that runs almost through the center of the passage. " But let my due feet never fail " is a frontier; what is north of it is unlike what is south.

The first seventeen lines of this concluding passage lead us back to " L'Allegro." " Such sights as youthful Poets dream / On Summer eves by haunted stream " collates in a way with the morning brook, the murmuring water, and the dream of " Il Penseroso," but the emphasis in counterdistinction is on youth, the beginning of things. Though similar, their dreams are not the same. The dream of " L'Allegro " is slighter in substance, common in poetic experience, and it leads to the sham reality of the theater and the " wanton heed " and " giddy cunning " of Lydian music. The dream of " Il Penseroso " is of a far higher order, a " strange mysterious dream " which is succeeded by a mysterious music, " above, about, or underneath." This music, unlike that which arouses Orpheus from his " golden slumber," cannot be identified or localized. It may be the music of the spheres. It may be the song of Apollo. The poet does not know. It is sent, perhaps, by a spirit to " mortals good "—*good* is, I expect, a master word—or by the genius of the place. The connections with the earlier passages are telling, but this section of the latter lines leads ineluctably to the conclusion.

The music is once again re-echoed in the music of the church which is neither natural nor inexplainable. The great polyphonic organ is above; the multivoiced quire is below; together they make the full throat of the universe. Verse and voice are married here. The ear is fully charged. The pictures—gifts to sight—are also identified. In the opening lines of this passage, portraits are laid softly on the eyelids of the sleeping poet; in the last lines these portraits become the "storied Windows richly dight" of the church. What was without reality in the earlier expression has shape and substance at the end. The common experience of the poet is transmogrified into a poetic experience that can be grasped by the aesthetic faculties. But the poet gets from the covert to the church through the "studious cloister." The cloister is the synonym for the tower in Milton's lexicon of symbols. The route of the progress is now mapped; common experience refined by intellectual experience makes for the highest sort of poetic experience. We are carefully informed that this is not ordinary poetic experience; the church, in a larger sense, assures an alteration of manner. In the church the theme of sight and sound, of pictures and music, unite in a powerful concluding succession.

> As may with sweetness, *through mine ear,*
> Dissolve me into extasies,
> And bring all Heav'n *before mine eyes.*

The universal music of the church, so unlike Lydian music or the strange tunes heard by the natural poet, effects a dream more profound and miraculous than that of the poet of " L'Allegro " or the " strange mysterious dream " with which the passage begins. " All Heav'n " takes the place of " Shallow Brooks, and Rivers wide." But there is still one more furlong in the journey.

Common experience, intellectual experience, poetic experience are not enough. The " Prophetic strain " is the child of " old experience," which is all of this experienced over and over again. The direction of the poems is that of a continued venture, and we must think of the poet as writing these poems tomorrow, the day after, and for years to come. As the Bear makes its relentless circle in the skies, the tireless poet must repeat this circle on earth and insatiately observe the ritual of the progress. When the final poem was written, the agony was finished because the way to the ultimate gratification was known, but there must be no slumber, no relapse into " loathed melancholy," only a ceaseless passing from one chamber of experience to the next.

II

THE HIGHER COMPROMISE:

"On the Morning of Christ's Nativity" and a Mask

I KNOW few better seventeenth century illustrations of an attempted reconciliation of opposites that failed than Milton's *Comus*. Beyond this, it is a superior example of poetic synthesis as it was understood at this time, and because of this, it has been only partially understood ever since. Yet, if we read the poem with an ear sensitive to catch the manifold nuances of the young Milton's already mature recollections, if we attempt to feel the poem with our sensibilities sharpened as much as they can be by the more central myths of that century, if we do all this and at the same time avoid the common inclination to regard the poem as a didactic allegory written by a precocious moralist, we shall see *Comus* as something quite different from what we thought it to be and we shall begin to understand Milton's ill success.

Unblinded by traditional preconceptions, we shall notice that this poem is an attempt to establish a *concors discors* on an elaborate scale, that it is essentially an attempted reconciliation of disparate parts, but since it is a frustrated reconciliation—one of those twisted intellectual-emotional experiences indigenous in this generation—it eventuates in confusion rather than in harmony. Unlike the eighteenth century, the age of Milton had not yet learned the fascination that the unharmonized juxtaposition of contraries has for the reasonable man. In its all too cursory pursuit of truth by the paradox, it did much to establish the rational methodology and even the aesthetic comportment of the Enlightenment, but I do not think that the men of this time employed the paradox with a conscious sense of system. For them the paradox was at one and the same time a form of youthful sophistry that could be catalogued as juvenilia and a keen implement of expository understatement; seldom was it a process, as it certainly was in the next century, of convicting oneself of orthodoxy. It was "a signe of admiration," [1] as Puttenham called it, rather than a test, as Cicero thought, " of whether a matter of worth to the learned has any common sense value." [2] But we shall be helped in unriddling the problem of *Comus* if, before we come to a close examination of the masque, we observe Milton's poetic procedure in his most perfect early work.

The conflict between the aesthetic and the intellectual daemons that fought for superior utterance in much of Milton's poetry may be first seen in the moving shadows of the " Nativity Ode." The theme is not original, nor is the poem, in spite of the epodic arrangement of the strophes, exactly an ode. Nevertheless, it is by far the most luxurious of English verses on the Incarnation in its erudition and the most sensitively felt. Before it, the prior offerings of Jonson, Drummond, and Beaumont fade into the commonplaceness of theological cliché. The more original poem of Southwell, which compresses its emotion within the narrow channels of gnomic expression, is companionable mainly in terms of a temperamental emblem. However, the power of this poem does not spring from a true reconciliation of its intellectual and emotional disunities, but rather from the fact that they are not reconciled at all, or, better still, that they are erased in a unity of a higher order. When we observe the conflict in its separateness, it seems like a tug-of-war between teams of gigantic stallions—the thesis and the antithesis pull oppositely, the synonym and antonym stretch each other, the myth dashes itself into divergent metaphors. That we accept the amazing procedure as artistically valid even to the extent that we overlook or apologize for such technical flaws as " When such musicke sweet," or the prolix roll call of the gods, or the

[1] *The Arte of English Poesie* (Cambridge, 1936), 226.
[2] *Paradoxa Stoicorum*, 4.

badly rendered metaphysical excesses, demonstrates the immediate and isolateral reaction of our own discordant organs of perception to this conflict. It is, to use a favorite Renaissance figure, as a struck lyre that sets all others in vibration. But a discord will do this as well as a harmony.

The " Ode " begins with an induction in which time is negated so that the discord between the past and the present, which we plainly understand, may be altered into a concord of eternity, or into an essence of time, which is timelessness. To this end the poem is carefully dated. The title and the induction inform us that it was written in the small hours of December 25, 1629. So that we shall be certain of this fact Milton reinforms us in the sixth elegy: " Illa sub auroram lux mihi prima tulit." This is a matter that Milton does not want the reader to miss because he is about to invent the fable that this fact is untrue, that the real time is the last hour of the pre-Christian era and that he is himself present in a land of palms and snow, a seventeenth century interloper between the events of the Nativity and the Epiphany. This is the temporal conflict, but what Milton does is to reconcile it by pressing towards the eternal consequences of the Incarnation. By annulling the chronology of this event, he extracts the everlasting from the conflict between the past and the present. This is the first higher compromise.

In the " Hymn " there are two central contentions: the minor dissonance between the two aspects of Nature, and the major dissonance between the two kinds of harmony. These contentions are emphasized by the fact that the " Hymn " falls naturally into three sections: stanzas I-VII, VIII-XVIII, and XIX-XXVIII. The symbolic narrative of the sun (embodying the pun familiar to Donne and Herbert) controls the movement of the first section and binds it to the time theme of the induction. As the paramour of pagan Nature, the sun introduces the theme of the first section, and as the discarded and abashed lover, staying in its road to re-emphasize the time motif of the induction, it makes a limitary conclusion. The contrast between the flagrancy of pagan Nature prior to the Incarnation and the subsequent shamefastness of the same personification is implied in the first two stanzas. The reconciliation here takes the form of Redemption. Nature, whose biography is that of the Magdalene—an intrinsically baroque identification—is redeemed by the greater Sun. Hence the redemption that arises from this conflict looks forward to the redemption of man in the latter stanzas, just as Peace, the instrument of the redemption, the *Concordia Christi*, looks ahead to the basic conflict between the ἁρμονία *Christianis* and the *consonantia pagana*. The rescue of Nature by the Peace of the greater Sun from the wanton embraces of the lesser sun is memorialized in the fifteenth stanza, for we know that she is to be registered among the daughters of God just as the woman taken in adultery was placed in the company of saints.

The conflict between Christian and pagan harmony that governs the second and third sections makes the " Hymn " an artistic wonder. Man enters at the beginning of the second section, but he enters to provide an audience for the sacred music which has not been heard since Eve succumbed to the blandishments of Satan. Man seems, in fact, to be almost out of place in this *dramatis personae* which is evenly divided between personified symbols and beings of a supernatural yet mythological order. But the interesting thing is not that man is attentive to the heavenly choir, but that Milton succeeds in effecting an artistic harmony while describing a spiritual disharmony. When he contemplates the difference between the pagan and the Christian world, he finds, like Plato's friend Archytas, a musical explanation. This is totally fitting, for Milton, as a good Graecist, certainly knew that the definition of ποιητής expunges the difference between poetry and music. Likewise he is not unaware that the *concordia* that he will now explicate poetically is the linguistic equivalent of the *pax* of the first section.

It is not surprising to discover that Milton's description of Christian harmony begins with a heraldic blending of clearly recognizable emblems: the circle, the globe, light. By the trick of the oxymoron they all become music, not a music of annotation but the essence of music. To this is joined the intermediate music of the spheres and the lower chant that the poet is composing. For Milton realized, as did the authors of the Psalms, that the music of the creatures was a required melody for the bass of Heaven's organ; and he knew, too, that at the moment of the Incarnation, the harmony was without flaw for the first time since the springtime of Creation. Distemperature comes again with the death of God and then the full music cannot be heard until after the Day of Wrath. This is the meaning of this section.

While the integral metaphor of Christian harmony as Milton conceived it has strong elements of pagan Pythagoreanism and while he must have known how often *concordia, consensus,* and *consonantia* appear as moral doublets in classical letters, yet he was unable, even while admiring, to perceive a premier harmony in the ancient philosophy that was the intellectual extension of pagan theology. Throughout his poetry, and especially in *Paradise Regained*, a discrimination is carefully made between Christian and pagan philosophy. Plato and Seneca are great thinkers and noble men when they stand against a non-Christian façade, but they dissolve into nothingness before the Christian revelation. We have, as a result, in the third section of the " Hymn," a pageant of gods drawn from the Old Testament and costumed by Selden.[3] They have their music, too, but it is a music best described by the "horrid clang" of the Last Judgment. The "Cymbals ring" and call " the grisly king "; and the "dismal dance," which is an awkward contrast to that of the angels, makes their ceremony more dreary.[4] These phrases, together with the cacophonous " Tim-

[3] The limiting descriptions of the gods probably comes from the *De dis Syris syntagmata II*, published a dozen years before this poem was written.

[4] The pertinent passage on the dance is *PL*, V. 618–27: That day, as other solemn days, they spent / In song and dance about the sacred Hill, / Mystical dance, which yonder starry Sphere / Of Planets and of fixt in all her Wheels / Resembles nearest, mazes intricate, / Eccentric, intervolv'd, yet regular / Then most, when most irregular they seem: / And in thir motions harmony Divine / So smooths her charming tones, that God's own ear / Listens delighted.

brel'd Anthems dark " of the devotees of Osiris, are inserted by Milton to suggest the nature of pagan music now " dumm " before the majesty of the Incarnate song. Hence from this conflict between the limited music of the Church Militant and the discordant melodies of pagan theology, Milton anticipates the multitoned yet perfectly matched harmony of the Church Triumphant. This is the third and greatest compromise.

The " Ode " has, then, three series of poetically expressed contrasts, and from each of them Milton draws a compromise that is far more splendid than the parts conflicting. From the variance between the past and the present, he extracts the solution of timelessness; from that between Nature abandoned and Nature redeemed, he creates a Nature as immutable and untarnished as Faith, Hope, and Peace; from the disagreement between pagan and Christian harmony, he derives the harmony of God. Underlying all of this is the conventional modulation of the universal and the particular which is signified by the movement from the abstract character of Peace to her concrete manifestations, a modulation that is also orchestrated by the epodic contraction and expansion of the metrical line. The result of this artistic procedure is a magnificent unity that greatly affects us.

This method of displaying the opposed unrealities and of drawing from the opposition a high poetic reality is a basic Miltonic technique. It is one of the more obvious methods of the greater poems, and the first two books of *Paradise Lost* afford us an important instance of its use. But Milton is not always successful in this process of bridging the chaos between opposed elements, and it is my contention that his failure to effect a compromise that is both poetically and intellectually greater than the warring opposites is what causes us so much trouble in the elucidation of *Comus*.

The conflicts in *Comus* are both extrinsic and intrinsic—in structure, in pre-texts, in theme, and in orchestration. They are conflicts that for many reasons Milton could not pacify by a higher compromise. For this reason the poem fails and we are baffled. To begin with, we should notice that the poem is not a masque at all. The bright critical eye of Samuel Johnson took this in at once. The poem, he said, is "deficient" as a drama. It is not a masque because it is not "given up to all the freaks of the imagination." The action, though human, is improbable and unreasonable. The dialogue is not composed of speeches but "declamations deliberately composed and formally repeated, on a moral question." The audience views the work, as a consequence, "without passion, without anxiety." "It is a drama in the epic style, inelegantly splendid and tediously instructive." [5]

All attempts to explain the exterior structure of *Comus* since 1780 have been answers to Dr. Johnson. Warton replied in a note prefixed to his edition of the *Poems*:

> We must not read Comus with an eye to the stage, or with the expectation of dramatic propriety. . . . Comus is a suite of Speeches, not interesting by discrimination of character; not conveying a variety of incidents, not gradually exciting curiosity; but perpetually attracting attention by sublime sentiment, by fanciful imagery of the richest vein, by an exuberance of picturesque description, poetical allusion, and ornamental expression. While it widely departs from the grotesque anomalies of the Mask now in fashion, it does not nearly approach to the natural constitution of a regular play, . . . This is the first time the old English Mask was in some degree reduced to the principles and form of rational composition. . . . On the whole, whether Comus be or be not deficient as a drama, whether it is considered as an Epic drama, a series of lines, a Mask, or a poem, I am of opinion, that our author is here only inferiour to his own Paradise Lost.[6]

Warton, as we see, is as obfuscated as Johnson. *Comus* is not a masque; it is not a play. It may be a drama in the epic style, a rational masque, a suite of verses, or a poem. It is in the last category that the nineteenth century placed the work and so avoided the issue about its structure. Macaulay thought of it as a series of " Majestic soliloquies " and lyrics that are spoiled

[5] *Lives of the English Poets* (Oxford, 1905), I, 168–69.
[6] *Op. cit.*, 262–63.

by the dramatic passages. " It is when Milton escapes from the shackles of the dialogue, when he is discharged from the labour of uniting two incongruous styles, when he is at liberty to indulge his choral raptures without reserve, that he rises even above himself." Macaulay is truly running for a safe wicket and Walter Bagehot is hard on his heels.

> *Comus* has no longer the peculiar exceptional popularity which it used to have. We can talk without general odium of its defects. Its characters are nothing, its sentiments are tedious, its story is not interesting. But it is only when we have realized the magnitude of its deficiencies that we comprehend the peculiarity of its greatness. Its power is in its style.[7]

The observations of Macaulay and Bagehot are, I think, born of an attempt to side-step the real problem of the external structure of *Comus*; yet in modern times we have gone still further and listed the poem among the moralities, contending that it is a sort of belated *Hickscorner* or *Lusty Juventus*. We have failed to notice the apologetic testimony of the Latin motto, or of the variants between the printed poem and the manuscripts which reflect Milton's own dissatisfaction with the work. Granted that we do not know a great deal about the masque and that those which we possess are essentially royal entertainments, still we must confess that *Comus* is so different from these as to be almost another thing. It is much longer than the masque as written by Jonson or Daniel; its cast of speaking characters is much smaller; its locale of action is much less fantastic; its plot, though not exactly more elaborate, is more tense; its theme is more serious; it is totally wanting in humorousness; and its emphasis is more on dramatic crisis than on spectacle, dance, costume, and even singing. We must also notice that it was given in a narrower hall than the great Jacobean masques, and that it concludes with a mock water pageant that is more properly part of an outdoor entertainment. The want of all these qualities disestablishes *Comus* as a true masque, although it does not make it into a drama. Nonethe-

---

[7] *Literary Studies* (London, 1879), I, 219.

less, I think we can say that Johnson was right and Warton wrong when the former criticized *Comus* as a drama and the latter denied the validity of this criticism.

To criticize *Comus* as a drama would be to do no more than extend Johnson's remarks, and Tillyard, who has as fine a sense of style as any academic critic of our time, has already made some telling observations about this problem. In addition, Tillyard has also very perceptively pointed out that the poetic texture of the masque is mixed in a fashion that suggests confusion rather than the more desirable quality of variety. *Comus*, as he sees it, is a sequence of poetical experiments. The subsurface technique is Arcadian, but there are also lapses into the manner of Elizabethan dramatists, into pastoral expression, into pure poetry, into Jacobean phrasing, and, in one of the excised manuscript passages, into Restoration realism.[8]

But the patchwork of styles does not, it seems to me, end here because the pallium of classical tragedy covers the whole poem. The masque opens with a prologuizer like Polydore's ghost of the *Hecuba*; and though we should expect the Lady and the Brothers—if the theme is what the commentators say it is—to enter next, we have instead the antistrophic choral of Comus which is a modified form of an antimasque. We then have the declamation of the Lady which ends with a lyric followed by the stichomythic section between her and Comus. Other remembrances of an antique nature assail us as we follow the unfolding of the masque, which concludes, we must admit, with as fine an example of the *deus ex machina* as any Athenian could devise. So in its external structure *Comus* is a mélange of various tendencies and styles that never merge into anything intensely organic.

Even if we admit that Milton was handicapped by the occasional requirements of the Bridgewater family and by the physical limitations of the hall in Ludlow Castle, I still cannot see that these restrictions necessarily resulted in attempts that fell short of compromise. Having previously written the *Ar-*

---

[8] *Milton* (London, 1934), 66–75.

cades, a true masque, Milton was not inexpert in the formal technique. Here he intended to transcend current practice by attempting to create a more dramatic form of short entertainment; and though *Comus* has held the stage better than any other masque, it is, nonetheless, an error in artistic judgment, for a conflict between exterior form and style seldom results in a valid compromise. From a compromise between a masque and a short musical drama, one gets either an unstylized masque or an undramatic play. We miss the formality and the ritual of the masque, and we have a play totally wanting in suspense and character alteration. This is the first attempted reconciliation in *Comus* and it fails; but the unsuccessful pursuit of artistic compromise is further verified by the two pre-texts upon which the theme is founded: the Circe story annotated by Peele's version of the Child Roland legend and modified by Spenser's account of Acrasia and Busyrane, and Geoffrey of Monmouth's eponymic history of Sabrina.

The Circe legend is introduced by the Spirit, who is really the Hermes of Homer in seventeenth century dress. The two brothers are composites of the Wandering Knight, of Ulysses, of Guyon, and of Britomart. Comus is, of course, the son and heir of Circe and the brother of Ariosto's Alcina, Trissino's Acratia, Tasso's Armida, and Spenser's mistress of the Bower of Bliss. The Circe story was authoritatively interpreted during the Renaissance as an allegory of the contention between Reason and Nature.[9] Spenser uses it in the Guyon story as an allegory of the conflict between Temperance and its opposite; whereas the story of the enchantment in the tale of Britomart is an allegory of chastity. The *Old Wives Tale*, which Milton follows so closely, has no special purpose beyond that of the satirically horrific. By attempting to unite all of these motifs with their diverse interpretations, Milton obtains a macaronic translation. We notice, too, that the Miltonic solution does not follow the traditional working-out of the pre-text. Ulysses subdues Circe; Guyon brings down the Bower of Bliss and traps the enchan-

[9] N. Comes, *Mythologiae libri* (Patavia, 1616), 309.

tress; Britomart breaks the power of Busyrane and rescues
Amoret. Even the Wandering Knight, assisted by the ghost of
Jack, procures the defeat and death of Sacrapant. The brothers,
though they have the Heaven-sent advice of the Spirit and the
Homeric moly, do not succeed so well as their literary pre-
cursors. Comus escapes with his crew of men-beasts; the Lady
remains frozen to her chair. The fact that Milton again is
trying to combine the masque and the drama makes in the case
of this pre-text an unsolved conflict between well-established
dramatic and allegorical traditions. Something not unlike this
happens to the pre-text of Sabrina.

I have a notion that when the masque was first commis-
sioned Milton intended to write a true masque based on the
Sabrina story. The Bridgewater estate was washed by a tribu-
tary of the Severn, and everyone living in the district must have
known how the river came by its name. Some years before the
masque was written, Drayton had elaborated the myth poetically in the *Poly-Olbion* and added a touch of pathos, suggested
perhaps by the account in the *Mirror for Magistrates*, to the
death of Locrine's natural daughter.[10] But the Sabrina of
Comus is not the Sabrina of Geoffrey of Monmouth or of Milton's later *History of Britain*. The story as Geoffrey and as,
subsequently, Milton recounts it is that Gwendolen, having
defeated Locrine and captured his mistress Estreldis and her
daughter Sabrina, caused the daughter, offspring of adultery, to
be cast in the river and ordered that thereafter the river be
called by the name of the unfortunate child.[11] Caught once
again by the requirements of the allegory and by the need for a
compliment, Milton is forced to change the first pre-text so that
he can bring in the Sabrina myth and then he is forced to alter
the myth to fit the revised first pre-text. In all previous accounts
except " The sad virgin innocent of all " of the second book of
the *Faerie Queene*, the emphasis is placed on the betrayal of
Gwendolen and this is Milton's emphasis in the *History of*

[10] *Works* (Oxford, 1933), IV. 114–15.
[11] See Geoffrey of Monmouth, II, 2–5; *History of Britain, Works* (New
York, 1932), X, 15.

Britain. Here it is changed. Sabrina becomes "a virgin pure" and a "guiltless dame" who, flying the "mad pursuit of her enraged stepdam," commends "her fair innocence" to the river. Milton converts what was thought to be history into saint's legend and governs it in part with the accounts of Circe's anointing of Ulysses and of Florimel in the sea caverns of Proteus. This modification, though suggestive, can only bother those who have the original history in their heads. It is the intellectual texture of the masque that baffles readers on all levels, and it is Milton's failure to bring about a higher compromise again that makes for this difficulty.

Although a number of essays have been written about *Comus*, Woodhouse [12] alone has made an intelligent attempt to untangle its meaning. In his cogently written study he describes the several floors of meaning that we should see in the masque. The central conflict, according to Woodhouse, is between Nature and Grace; Temperance and Continence are the virtues rallied under the first, Virginity under the second. Sharing in both and connecting them in this pagan-Christian duel is the essential doctrine of Chastity. There is, I think, little doubt about the correctness of most of Woodhouse's analyses, but again no effective compromises are made and it does not seem to me that Milton's artistic emphasis coincides with his intended moral emphasis. A close examination of the broad structure of the dramatic movement is likely to support this contention.

After the opening chorals, the two brothers enter. The Second Brother is in a fret for fear that his sister has fallen victim either to the hunger of an animal or the lust of a wild man. "Within the direful grasp / Of savage hunger, or of savage heat?" The First Brother hypothesizes on the nature of her virtue and recommends the wilderness as a place for moral contemplation. The Second Brother admits that all of this may be true for the lonely anchorite, but he reminds his elder that the Lady is beautiful and, consequently, a desirable prey for the incontinent. The First Brother says that she has hidden

[12] "The Argument of Milton's Comus," *University of Toronto Quarterly* (1941–42), XI, 46–71.

strength, and the Second Brother asks whether this is the strength of Heaven. The First Brother then lectures on chastity and virginity, virtues defended by both classical allusions and angelic guardians. His homily is belied almost at once by the Spirit, who—in spite of his announcement in the prologue that he is sent as the " defence and guard " of wanderers in Comus' territory—is forced to report that the Lady has fallen into the hands of Circe's son before he could prevent it. The brothers are now told how to overcome Comus, but it is shortly made obvious that the Second Brother's original fears are sound. Comus escapes unpunished with all his creatures, and the Lady is finally released not because of her virginity or through the offices of just one of " the thousand liveried angels " but through the magic powers of a pagan water spirit, whose myth was renovated and carpentered for this purpose.

The failure of this part of *Comus* to come off according to promise is further complicated by Milton's unsuccessful attempt to establish a true intellectual conflict in the debate between Comus and the Lady. This is, without question, the most dramatic part of the poem and I am quite ready to agree with Johnson that " it wants nothing but a brisker reciprocation of objections and replies to invite attention and detain it." Its effectiveness as a dramatic episode is destroyed by a double flaw. Though it starts out with a certain amount of dramatic excitement, the scene quickly degenerates into a philosophic dialogue as eclectic as one of the dialogues of Cicero, and the initial excitement is immediately quieted by the fact that we know almost at once that there is not the remotest danger of the Lady's accepting the offer of Comus. The ethical premises of the debate are, in the second place, so mixed that the intellectual colors run together and are never well marked. Comus adopts a modified Neo-Epicurean argument that is reminiscent of all humanistic debates on this matter. For this we are hardly prepared since he had earlier been charmed by the Lady's song of " all Heaven's harmonies," "a sober certainty of waking bliss," and had talked of making her his queen. This is as fine a prospect of irrational miscegenation as one is likely to find in the history of marriage. The Lady, in her turn, meets the first half of Comus's proposition with statements that he properly labels as "stoic," and she repels the second half with the quasi-Christian concept of virginity. She is a curious mixture, half-rational, half-intuitive; human she is, indeed, but hardly the banner-bearer of her creed. Her character, like that of Comus, also undergoes a forest-change, for the innocent young maiden of the early poem becomes a *mulier doctissima* with the stern frigidity of an adolescent Isabella. And all of this occurs within the space of a gasp.

We feel that if Comus had preserved his character, he could neatly have countered the Lady's objections with the realistic premise of a Valla: "Nullum in rebus humanis intolerabilius virginitate tormentum est."[13] He does, in fact, almost get to this, but his former crystal-like lucidity breaks down and he becomes almost as dogmatically objectionable as the Lady herself.

> Come, no more,
> This is mere moral babble, and direct
> Against the canon laws of our foundation;
> I must not suffer this, yet 'tis but the lees
> And settlings of a melancholy blood;
> But this will cure all straight, one sip of this
> Will bathe the drooping spirits in delight
> Beyond the bliss of dreams (806–13).

The spinsterish tone of Comus jars us, so we are not surprised in the end when he falls back on the formula of the official Christian tempter and says, "Be wise and taste." Nonetheless, if dramatic logic had been allowed to control this scene, Comus would have made his point. The Lady's victory seems as much a tour de force as the final half-Christian, half-Platonic admonition of the departing Spirit.

Denis Saurat put his finger on the central difficulty when he wrote: "There is little that is Christian about *Comus*."[14]

---

[13] D. C. Allen, "The Rehabilitation of Epicurus," *SP*, XLI (1944), 7.
[14] *Milton: Man and Thinker* (New York, 1925), 16.

That is a reasonably accurate observation, and yet in recent times the masque has been too often read as a treatise on Christian morals. The virtues celebrated in the poem, as Milton and any other seventeenth century man knew, are Christian only by adoption. Both the sixteenth and seventeenth centuries were aware that Virtue existed before Grace. They frequently noticed that among the pagans there were temperate nations like Sparta, temperate classes like the Magi, and many temperate individuals like Plato and Seneca. Any Englishman of this intemperate English era could also recount the virtuous lives of the chaste Penelope, Lucretia, Sophronia, Zenobia, and Timoclea, or the virginal Biblia, Daria, Spurina, and Euphrosyna. So the core of the theme is Christian only in terms of a special modern prejudice.

If the theme is not unspottedly Christian, the time of the action is not necessarily fixed in the calendar limits of Christianity. The temporal circumstances are set by the myths of Sabrina and Comus. Sabrina was the granddaughter of Brute; she lived a generation after the fall of Troy and a great time before the birth of Christ. Though the dramatic time is nowhere stated, there is every reason to believe that Milton thought of the action as taking place in pre-Christian Albion. The Spirit, for example, is not a guardian angel but a daemon (as he is called in the Trinity MS) from the *Timaeus*. He comes from " the starry threshold of Jove's court," talks constantly of the pagan pantheon, of nymphs of wood and stream, and, when he finally leaves the stage, goes off to a pagan paradise. Comus is no refugee from Pandæmonium but a true son of Circe and Bacchus—notice how contemporaneous he is with Sabrina—who is well-acquainted with the upperclass members of the pagan underworld. The Lady and her brothers spend most of their time in a pre-Christian ambient and their conversation is studded with classical mythology. When the First Brother wishes to illustrate his lecture on chastity, he calls "Antiquity from the old schools of Greece " and tells us about Minerva and Diana and not about the martyrs of the Primitive Church. So the dial of the dramatic clock tells pagan time.

But Milton refuses to maintain the obvious chronology. He tries for a temporal compromise by scattering Christian metaphors through the masque in order to accent the utilitarian fiction—as indicated by the first speech of the Spirit and the second or presentation song—that all of this actually happened to the Bridgewater children on their way to join their parents. This is a conflict similar to that of the " Ode," but it cannot be compromised by means of unassimilated Christian metaphors. The two chronological divisions simply cannot be poured together and their metaphors confuse the careful reader. Though the characters in general speak like pagans, they momently become Christian. The Spirit uses expressions like " sainted seats " and " sin-worn "; Comus mentions " the path to Heaven "; the First Brother capitalizes " Heaven " and refers to armored "angels "; and the Second Brother comes out with a Roman turn of phrase: " For who would rob a hermit of his weeds, / His few books, or his beads, or maple dish." The Lady has most of the metaphors: "soft votarist in palmer's weeds," " Conscience," " Faith," " Hope," " hovering Angel," " He, the Supreme God," who " would send a glistering guardian, if need were, / To keep my life and honour unassailed." Instead of effecting a higher compromise, this method leads us to believe that the characters are uncertain about their theology and their chronology. But, perhaps, I have missed the real point of the masque.

In the printed and manuscript versions the title is " A Mask presented at Ludlow Castle." This may come as a surprise to some readers because the earliest critics refer to it as *Comus* and few modern Miltonists think of it under any other title. The reason for this is clear; the character of Comus dominates the masque whether Milton intended it or not. One cannot imagine *Macbeth* if it were untitled getting the popular title of *MacDuff*, or *Hamlet* becoming *Claudius*. Likewise if Milton's theme of chastity had been firmly brought home, this masque might be known as *The Mask of Chastity* or *The Mask of the Virgin*. There is, I believe, a reason for this.

Though chastity or temperance triumphs in the masque, the

motif that is really dramatically interesting is the process of temptation. This is a theme dear to Milton's heart and one which he elaborated in all of his later works. If we can assume that the time is pre-Christian, *Comus* takes its place as part of a great poetic tetralogy. In *Paradise Lost* we witness temptation at the beginning of things in heaven, in hell (the temptation of Sin), and on earth. In *Samson Agonistes* we see the temptation of a foreshadower of Christ under the Old Law and how it was withstood. In *Paradise Regained* we watch the temptation of " the exalted man " and the ordination of the New Dispensation. In *Comus* we are spectators at a pagan temptation. From all of these vicarious experiences we can draw lessons for our own guidance. The masque seems to me to be an experimental piece in this respect, a prolegomenon to the three great poems. But the conflict between the dramatic theme and the moral theme is never made quite clear and it is certainly never, in my estimation, artistically compromised.

Because the conflicts of the " Ode " eventuate in higher compromises, whereas in the masque the conflicts in external structure, in pre-text, and in thematic substance continue to struggle for an equation that cannot be written, the " Ode " satisfies us aesthetically and the masque does not. The history of *Comus* among the critics suggests that Milton was unable to convey his meaning through a dramatic form; hence it is probably a good thing that " Adam Unparadiz'd " became *Paradise Lost*. Perhaps Milton learned something from his experience with *Comus*.

III

THE TRANSLATION OF THE MYTH:

The Epicedia and "Lycidas"

*P*INDAR'S affective phrase Σκιᾶς ὄναρ ἄνθρωπος is a worthy motto for the shield of most Christian warriors of the seventeenth century. When I say this I am innocent of irony, for though the shield might be the " *scutum fidei* " of St. Paul, the arm that sustained it shook only too often with what has been called " the metaphysical shudder." Death and the grave—at once mistress and bed—dwelled so hungrily on the margins of existence that we, in our infidelity, are sometimes amazed that men of such strong Christian resolution should be always preoccupied with the cringing anticipation of an event that ought truly to be the beginning of the Christian experience. Perhaps it is for this reason—the notion of death as the antechamber of the real life—that men of this generation were so obsessed with the anacoluthic moment in their biography, for we also learn from their preserved contemplations that they nourished an assurance of continuation. The tolling bell could be converted by the miracle of divine harmony into the happy chime of marriage. Yet somehow, at this temporal distance, we feel that the process of the conversion, save in the texts of the mystics, is one of reason and will, a Christian variation on the last moments of the *Phaedo*. So neglecting for a moment the rhetorical tradition, we ponder the intensity of belief.

It would be trite to say that this whole phenomenon is a baroque nuance, and yet it is so important to say this that I beg the indulgence of repetition. The baroque can be defined only in architecture with any precision, and yet we can possibly say that it is the underlayer of mediaeval emotions which became visible again as the surface of Renaissance rationalism was weathered away. There is, however, an alteration in surface provoked by an understanding of spiritual reasonableness which the Middle Ages did not customarily have. To comprehend this almost evasive shift in emotion, we should remember the variations in the symbol of mortality, the sepulchral monument. The reclining mediaeval knight—Sir John Newton of Yatton or Sir Richard Choke of Long Ashton—whom the effigy-makers endowed with all the physical attributes of slumber, becomes on occasion in the early Renaissance a nude cadaver, shrunken and parched, but not yet gone to bone. The bone comes later: first as a decorative detail of Renaissance sarcophagi; then, by the time of the high baroque, that which was but an embellishment for pediment and panel burgeons into the emergent form of skeletal Death, poising his dart at the victim who cowers within the vainly protecting arms of a friend or relative. Death triumphs in his threat and it is man who stands between the fainting prey and the merciless hunter.

Imperial Death appears in all of his baroque ornateness as a titanic character in *Paradise Lost*, but the aging poet had long meditated the monster's insatiable appetite for the world's flesh and written a number of epicedia before he drew his final epic personification of "the meager Shadow." Five of these exercises were composed in his eighteenth year, and it is interesting, but totally fitting, that in his earliest poetry he should have gone promptly to the central problem of the baroque. The compelling force, I am certain, was artistic rather than morbid, but we must also recall that it is at this time of life, the very beginning, as it is, of human experience, that the inexorable aspects of death are most clearly, most horribly discerned by sensitive young men. Yet when Milton sought to examine this inner dread by means of a certain genre of poetry, he was caught at once in the torrent of a great tradition and was forced to struggle with all the strength of his young talent. Before we can weigh the talent, we must know the tradition.

Since philosophy is essentially the raw material of consolation and since its primary end is the explanation of death, it is not surprising that the beginnings of this type of poetic expression go back to the optimistic remarks of Socrates who was simply extending the prior ideas of Democritus. On this subject no post-Platonic philosopher is silent, and all their ameliorating arguments were finally put together by the rhetorician Krantor in a book that is now lost. " It is not a large book," Cicero writes, " but a golden one . . . it must be memorized to the last word." [1] Milton, like Cicero, took counsel with his great predecessors; but even as a young man, he must have been aware of a blending of patterns.[2]

As early as the time of Menander of Laodicea, the paramythia had been formularized into rhetorical logoi that enabled the man of letters to convert the works and days of his fellows into myths like those of the gods. The work, we are told, should begin with a lamentation; then it should mention the ancestry (γένος), the character (φύσις), the rearing and education (ἀνατροφή καὶ παιδεία), and the career and major exploits (ἐπιτηδεύματα καὶ πράξεις) of the deceased. It must end with arguments against mourning and remind the sorrowers that the one for whom they weep is in Elyzium.[3] The poetic variation comes in the standard topoi against mourning which provided the Greek and Latin consolatory writers with unlimited modes of expression. Death we learn from most consolationes is an expected and unavoidable debt owed Nature, a debt that no man can escape paying. We are also told that it releases us from earthly troubles and the yearning for earthly delights.

---

[1] Academica, 2. 135.

[2] See C. Buresch, " Consolationum a graecis romanisque scriptarum historia critica," Leipziger Studien, IX (1887), 1–169; C. Martha, Etudes morales sur l'antiquité, Paris, 1883; S. Mary Evaristus, The consolations of death in ancient Greek Literature, Washington, D. C., 1917; S. Mary Fern, The Latin consolatio as a literary type, St. Louis, 1941. For a limited study of Renaissance method see B. Boyce, " The stoic consolatio and Shakespeare," PMLA, LXIV (1949), 771–80.

[3] Περὶ ἐπιδεικτικῶν, Rhetores Graeci (Lipsiae, 1856), III, 412–14.

Sorrow is the best purge of sorrow; yet it is unnatural to grieve overlong. Man is made into a myth, but there is lamentation for what was once man and consolation for those who await their own metamorphoses.

What the pagan rhetoricians could formulate so precisely, the Christian rhetoricians could adapt and revise for the comfort of those who stood weeping about a saintly bier. There are some excellent witnesses to this in the funeral orations of Gregory Nazianzen; his best is, perhaps, his paramythia on his brother Caesar. Gregory was an accomplished rhetorician (he tells us that he was sent to the Palestinian schools because of his "too great love of rhetoric"), and so he begins with a Christianized lamentation. He describes his brother's Christian parents (γένος), his enlightened character (φύσις), his Alexandrian education (παιδεία), and his rapid rise in both the medical profession and the affairs of state (ἐπιτηδεύματα καὶ πρᾶξεις) . To underline the latter, he writes a brilliant excursus on his brother's heroic deeds during the earthquake at Nicaea. He follows thus far the prescriptions of the rhetors and he should now make some reference to the fields of the Hereafter, quoting, if he liked, from the speeches of Sophocles' Antigone or Euripides' Admetus. But Gregory is not a pagan, so this is his most extensive and glorious section, which is at once both a compound of Christian idealism and of the elder metaphors that sounded so nobly in the mouths of Cicero, Plutarch, or Seneca.

The pagan paramythia becomes a Christian consolation when Gregory says that Caesar has gone beyond the skies where he hears the angelic choir and sees the shining societies of the blessed. Since he has come at last to the pure fount of knowledge, all pleasures and prizes of the earth are worthless. But what is life itself except a meditation of death when it is compared to eternity?

> From these few days that remain to us shall we not make this gain that we shall see, endure, and perhaps commit more evil. Finally, we shall pay tribute to Nature's firm and stable law. We shall follow some and precede others; we shall

mourn for some and be mourned. The gain of tears that we shall pay to some, shall be repaid by others.

Here is an ancient rhetorician who has seen the light of God. He could preach in St. Paul's. He could write *Holy Dying*. Gregory continues in what seems to be a familiar vein, but it is familiar because we have heard its echoes in seventeenth century literature. Life, he says, is a child's game, a shadow that cannot be held, a bird going by on the wing, a ship leaving no track in the sea, a vapor, the dew of the morning, a flower blossoming and withering. Vanitas! Vanitas! " And so we do not weep for Caesar, who awaits the resurrection, but for ourselves who are left behind." Now he fears no tyrant, hoards no treasure, dreads no envy. No longer need he read useless Hippocrates and Galen; no longer need he expound senseless Euclid or Ptolemy; no longer need he confute the illogical philosophers. No longer! No longer! " Some will say—I expect that Gregory paused here—that now he can never receive his patrimony. But what cares he? He has his great inheritance." ῍Ω τῆς καινῆς παραχλήσεως: " O new consolation." [4] With this exclamation Gregory breaks with the tradition of pagan rhetoric. It is this Christian redaction of the classical methods of discourse that accounts in part for the elegies of Milton; and for a western counterpart of Gregory we can turn to Jerome, whose celebrated epistle to Heliodorus on the death of Nepotian is a key text.[5]

As all fathers of the Church prior to the sixth century, Jerome was trained in the classical gymnasia and wrote in high consciousness of the rhetorical tradition. He informs us that he had read the books that Krantor wrote to console his

---

[4] " Oratio in laudem Caesarii fratris," *PG*, XXXV, 755–87.

[5] *Epistulae* (Vienna, 1910), 548–75. See also Ambrose, *De excessu fratris sui Satyri* and *De obitu Valentiniani consolatio, PL*, XVI, 1340–1443; Cyprian, " Ad Turasium Presbyterum," *PL*, IV, 447–52; and Fulgentius, " Ad Gallam," *PL*, LXV, 311. Augustine's " Ad sanctum filiam Sapidam," *PL*, 1082–84 is an interesting combination of a consolation and a manual on Christian widowhood.

grief, the books that " Cicero imitated," as well as the consolatory works of Plato, Diogenes, Clitomachus, Carneades, and
Posidonius. He knows the formularies but he despises them.

> The advice of the rhetoricians in such matters is that you
> should first find out the ancestors of the person to be praised
> and tell their deeds and come by steps to your subject so as
> to make him more famous by his paternal virtues so that it
> may be seen that he has not degenerated from the worth of
> his forefathers or perhaps has added splendor to an ordinary
> family. But as I am required to sing the praises of the soul,
> I shall not dwell on the fleshly renown which Nepotian
> himself contemned.

The earthly career is nothing; the conventional paramythia
fails now because the emphasis must be placed on the consolatory topic of the higher life. Jerome tells, of course, about
Nepotian's career as a soldier of the court and of his supreme
piety and charity after he put off the sword belt and became
a soldier of Christ, but the themes of Menander cease with
this, for a new topos intrudes—the topos of a quiet and holy
deathbed. Few pagan paramythia can tell of this; no pagan
can scorn it. For " the pagan dies out of his glory, the Christian
into his ": " Ille moriturus ex gloria est, iste moritur semper
ad gloriam."

The epistle to Heliodorus concludes with a topic that is
not unknown to the pagan rhetoricians: death is a release from
sorrow. Gregory had made use of this theme and his coeval
Jerome elaborates it. In his death Nepotian has not only
escaped from the terrors of an age in which both the Empire
and the Christian community are being ravaged by the bar-
barians but also from all the individual sorrows and cares by
which mortals are afflicted. The lot of the Christian, Jerome
exclaims, is alone made tolerable through the *caritas* of Christ.
" Haec semper vivit in pectore; ob hanc Nepotanius noster
absens praesens est et per tanta terrarum spatia divisos utraque
conplectitur manu." The pagan may complain of life; the
revered Krantor may say that it " is a punishment, and to be

born a human being, the highest peak of calamity "; [6] but they cannot say what Jerome has said. *Caritas* spares us and the sure knowledge that the Christian dead, though separated from us by an immensity of space, can reach across it and take us by the hand resolves time into eternity. And it all is ours " Through the dear might of him that walk'd the waves." This, too, is the great new consolation.

This *contaminatio* of pagan and Christian topoi in the mode of the paramythia lies behind all of Milton's elegies and it is seen immediately in his poetic exercise, " On the Death of a Fair Infant," which may be a poem begotten by his first intimate experience with death. Warton saw the artistic qualities of this poem when he described it as an " extraordinary effort of fancy, expression, and versification " in which the youthful poet demonstrates " his ability to succeed in the Spenserian stanza." [7] But the poem is more than this; it is a vivid indication of the poet's mature technique.

We must notice that Milton is faced with a poetic problem that no previous writer of poetry of this sort had been forced to solve. Other poets—Statius for example—had written on the death of children, but in each instance the subject was old enough to reveal what Menander called φύσις. Milton's infant had hardly breathed. A more experienced poet might have addressed the poem to the child's mother; but Milton, after an opening that is traditional, invents the fiction that he can converse with the dead, that the hand has reached across space. To make the achievement of the poem still more difficult, he refrains from blending pagan and Christian myths, separating them by a poetic barrier that is central to the poem. In this way he avoids the usual Christian apology, for most of the fathers who use such devices introduce them with timid phrases. By neither blending nor apologizing for these intrusions, Milton gives to his poem a horizontal movement of three tenses, the past, the present, and the future and a vertical movement

[6] *Fragmenta philosophorum Graecorum* (Paris, 1860–81), Frag. 12.
[7] *Poems upon Several Occasions* (London, 1791), 294.

from heaven to earth, from *here* to *there*. Though clumsy in movement, the poem is never static.

If we are at all aware of classical symbols, the opening lines tell us at once that we are in the past and that we are about to hear a *lamentatio* over someone who died too young.

> O fairest flower no sooner blown but blasted,
> Soft silken Primrose fading timelessly.

Since the time of Todd, this opening statement has been anchored to the first quatrain of the tenth sonnet of *The Passionate Pilgrim*, and it also looks forward to " Bring the rathe primrose that forsaken dies." The Shakespearean phrase may have echoed in Milton's heart; but the youth who had been made familiar with classical tropes at St. Paul's must have known that he stood on ancient soil. The quickly fading rose is a symbol that dominates epitaphic verse, and the primrose that sprung from the blood of the young Adonis as the aenemone that grew from Aphrodite's tears (Ἇιμα ῥόδον τίκτει, τὰ δὲ δάκρυα τὰν ἀνεμώναν) [8] is a perpetual emblem of those who died before their time. It is significant, too, that the companion flowers of Bion's poem are joined with the hyacinth in the epitaph that Moschus composed in his behalf, for a remembrance of these phrases conducts us, as it may have led Milton, to the legend of Hyacinthus in the fourth stanza. Yet, although the primrose fades timelessly, its symbolism detains us in the past, for Milton, truly inexperienced in a worldly sense and totally unmindful of personal loss, does not attempt to reduce the symbol by Renaissance idiom to a topic of consolation as Malherbe does in his " Consolation a M. du Perier." It remains as a mythic catalyst.

Since the infant has no mythology, she must be made a

---

[8] Bion, " Lament for Adonis," 66. For Milton, Horace had probably stated best its flowery evanescence: "et nimium brevis/flores amoenae ferre iube rosae" (*Car.* 2. 3. 13–14), but he may have known its funeral aspects best in the Propertian: " Molliter et tenera poneret ossa rosa" (Cynthia, 1. 17. 22).

myth by simile; hence the illusion of the antique is further extended by two familiar myths that are associated with the legend of the rose. The child was dead in a cold month, so Milton feigns that she has become the bride of Winter. Ovid describing the rape of Orithyia by Boreas writes the consolatory summation: " Illic et gelidi coniunx Actaea tyranni." [9] Now Winter, says Milton, has caught you in his " cold-kind " embrace. Catachresis makes the point and elevates an English infant to an Athenian princess.

Made brave by this invention, the imagination of the poet moves immediately to another legend of Boreas that elaborates the mythic mood of the epicedium. In the commentary of Servius on Vergil's third eclogue, he read that it was Boreas, not the more familiar Zephyr, who diverted the discus of Apollo and gave Hyacinthus his mortal wound. So we get to the second myth through the associative symbol of the first. The " silken primrose " produces the " purple flower " just as surely as the jealousy of Winter at the love-fortune of Aquilo begets the jealousy of Boreas at the love-fortune of Apollo. At this point the structure of the poem changes. The *lamentatio* with which the poem begins and the implied paramythia of the double myth becomes an epicedium with the proclamatory line: " Yet I cannot persuade me thou art dead."

The stylized paramythia of the classical period often ended with a brief description of the higher life of the deceased pegged on the end as a final note of praise or consolation. Plutarch reminds Apollonius that his son is now " feasting with the gods and would not be satisfied with your course of life." [10] Ovid describes Tibullus as enjoying the company of Catullus and Calvus in the Elysian Fields; [11] whereas the elegant consolatory poet Statius assures his friend Flavius Ursus that the slave boy whom he mourns " has joined the Blessed and enjoys the quiet of Elyzium." " Perhaps," he adds, " he will meet his famous

[9] *Metamorphoses*, 6. 711. Milton prefers the Latin *Aquilo*.
[10] *Consolation to Appollonius*, 37.
[11] *Amores*, 3. 10. 59–66.

ancestors there or besides the sweet silence of Lethe, the
Avernal nymphs play about him and Proserpine recognizes
him with a sidelong glance." [12] More magnificent by far than
all other pagan accounts of the life after death is the concluding
section of Seneca's *Ad Marciam*, a section that was perhaps
the model for a dozen hexameters of the later " *Naturam non
pati senium*," and we are not surprised that after the Renaissance had read it the fiction of Seneca's conversion to Christianity got abroad.

Milton is most aware of this topical obligation and in his
subsequent epicedia he consistently comments on the conditions of the new life. In the third elegy he dreams of a classical
Elyzium through which Bishop Andrewes walks and listens to
the " celestial ranks clapping their jewelled wings." A similar
vision is implied in the " *In obitum praesulis Eliensis*," and
the vice-chancellor is accorded the pious wish that he, too, may
wander in the immortal Fields. This ordinary conclusion is
refabricated according to the manner of Dante and Petrarch in
the epitaph on the Marchioness of Winchester.

> There with thee, new welcome Saint,
> Like fortunes may her soul acquaint,
> With thee there clad in radiant sheen,
> No Marchioness, but now a Queen.

It would have been odd had Milton not employed this topic
in this early English elegy, but the variation that he uses is
mythic and hence adjusted to the tenor of the whole poem.

The concluding couplet of the dubitative fifth stanza leads
directly to the double question of stanza six. " Are you in
Heaven [and it is the Heaven of Dante] or are you in the
Elysian Fields? " and " Were you mortal? " On the answer
to these two inquiries, the remainder of the poem is con-
structed. The first question is answered by avoiding it, for
it is put as a rhetorical question to permit the poet to answer
the second question in the negative. This lyrical negative is

fashioned of a second series of myths which are interchangeable yet made discrete by the stanzaic divisions. In the eighth stanza, however, they flow together as the Christian truth absorbs the honest verities of paganism.

The first myth is that of the Gigantomachia (not the less justifiable war with the Titans as some commentaries have it), the almost intolerable conflict between good and evil, concord and discord, that looks forward to the war on the plains of Heaven. For this Milton drew on Ovid or, perhaps, on Apollodorus whom he had read at St. Paul's.[13] The phrase "shak't Olympus" pins the legend down. But the soul of the infant, if it were a star, could not have fallen during this mythological assault which was too long ago. A recent attack on Heaven with poetic rather than chronological limits must be postulated, a more vigorous attack during which a goddess fled. But no goddess fled Heaven as Astrea fled earth.[14] Milton now has his poetical gambit and Ovid has probably helped him by describing the flight of Astrea immediately before the Gigantomachia in the *Metamorphoses*. The star also has its place, for the fleeing Astrea is translated into the sign Virgo.

The pieces of the myth now come together—a fallen star, the two attacks on Heaven, a goddess in flight, Astrea or Justice—and advance precisely towards a pair of abstract summations. The final personification begets the copula of allegorical abstractions common to pagan and Christian thought; " Mercy (?) [15] that sweet smiling Youth " and " white-robed Truth " follow in the train of Justice and the grand parade is closed by the " golden-winged host " of stanza IX, which evokes the remembrance of many Christian stories. Pagan myth, with Christian undertones, leads to universal philosophical abstractions that open the door to Christian legend. This congeries of myths,

---

[13] *The Library*, I. 6. 1–2, or Regius' comment on Ovid.

[14] See mentions of Astrea in Prolusion IV and Elegy IV.

[15] So emended by Heskin in 1750. I would suggest " Virtue " whom the pagans considered the child of Truth; see Gyraldus, *Syntagma deorum*, in *Opera* (Leyden, 1696), I, 27–28.

interwoven, hopelessly tangled, is for a modern swollen and pompous, but it is truly not indecorous if we accept the central hypotheses of the baroque.

The remaining stanzas are an epitome of the traditional *consolatio*. The child died during an epidemic which she is now asked to dispel, and for a moment we are reminded of Statius' lines on the death of Priscilla.[16] The topic is also reminiscent of the Christian doctrine of the potent presence of the hallowed death, a topic second in importance only to that of higher life. But by this time Milton was so caught in his own mythical web that he was unable to make the traditional distinctions. Having earlier changed the infant into a goddess, he now prays to her as if she were a saint; then he appends an inartistic consolation in brief, a commonplace compilation, that is addressed to the mother. This final stanza is a poetical imperfection since it not only diverts the direction of the poem from the child to the mother but ends in an incoherent and confusing couplet. Had Milton been able at this point to intensify his feelings or to strengthen the emotional impact of his lines, the poem might have been more successful. As it is, he builds up to nothing. His own emotions were hardly involved and he ended the poem to be done with it.

The subsequent elegies are similar in technique and in emotionlessness. With the exception of the monody on Jane Savage, these exercises are in Latin; and in spite of occasional powerful lines predicting the later Milton, they are little better than school tasks. The Hobson poems are the final winding out of this game. They are scherzos which suggest not only the poet's growing skill but his increasing weariness. The difficulty is that nothing was felt, that they were all set-pieces on subjects at hand. The emotion came after the poet had a fuller sense of his own prospects.

The intensity of feeling that we miss in Milton's earlier poems bursts forth at last in " Lycidas," which is not only a

---

[16] *Silvae*, 5. 155–69.

farewell to a dead friend but, in a half-suspected way, to his own dedicated career. Behind it lies a decade of experience and preparation that the poet of the earlier poems lacked, and in this case there was an immediacy of impulsion that drew the heart as well as the brain into the poetic mesh. " Lycidas " which seems at first to be little more than a forced oblation arises from a consciousness of mortality that possessed the poet in a fateful year. Sara Milton died in the spring of 1637, and in the fall, close to the time of King's death in the Irish Sea, the great Ben Jonson was carried to his narrow grave in the Abbey amid the rhythmic laments of all the minor poets in Britain. Neither of these greater deaths resulted in a poem, but the ground was prepared so that when the old Cantabs decided to memorialize the death of King in a collection of verses, " Lycidas " came forth on order, as it seems, but really not on order at all. It is a poem from the deep heart's core, and it must be regarded in this way or it cannot be understood at all.

To an age in which an immodest modesty is the cachet of a well-disciplined artist, Milton's continual announcements from his twentieth year onward of his plans to devote his life to letters seem at once naive and egocentric. We must recognize, however, that this type of confession is central to Christian humanism in its best form, and that it is compounded of the mediaeval surrender to God and the Renaissance surrender to art. It is a perfect exfoliation of the program that Erasmus laid down for the humanists of northern Europe. So when Milton speaks of his poetic purpose in the sixth and seventh prolusions, when he describes his impatience with his literary ripeness in " A letter to a Friend," when after the writing of *Comus* he proclaims his greater duties in the seemingly unfilial " Ad Patrem," or when he writes to Diodati in September, 1637: " And what am I doing? Growing my wings and meditating flight; but yet our Pegasus raises himself on very tender pinions "—when he does all this, he is speaking the dialect of his age. The " Epitaphium Damonis " is one witness to what the plans were, but even when poetry must be abandoned, when the ideal must go down before the actual, hope is still clutched with ever-slipping fingers, and the great task is still half-seen through the dusk of the immediate.

> Then, amidst the hymns and hallelujahs of saints, someone may perhaps be heard offering at high strains in new and lofty measures to sing and celebrate Thy divine mercies and marvellous judgments in this land throughout the ages, whereby this great and warlike nation, instructed and inured to the fervent and continual practice of truth . . . may press on hard to that high and happy emulation to be found the soberest, wisest, and most Christian people at that day, when Thou, the eternal and shortly expected king, shall open the clouds to judge the several kingdoms of the world. . . .[17]

This is an apex of intent, and with it Milton's steady progress towards universality is made manifest. It is no wonder that the history of Englishmen was eventually abandoned for that of Christmen, that Prince Arthur capitulated to God.

But to return to "Lycidas." Edward King, an old college friend, a cleric with slight poetic gifts, perishes. A small quarto of verse in Greek, Latin, and English is gathered in his memory. None of the poems save one is really worth the reading, and, as is usually the case, the poet brings up the rear. "Lycidas" stands at the end, a St. Michael of the guarded mount, and thereafter it stands before all English elegies. To explain its permanency and force, we can begin by asking questions and the first of these concerns Milton's reason for choosing the pastoral mode.

Though academic critics have been tireless in commenting on the Greek and Latin tradition that governs Milton's latter English elegy and have almost swamped the poem in a morass of analogues, it is not a literary tradition alone—granting that it plays a part and one quite different from that indicated by some commentaries—that impelled him to give up the tight

---

[17] *Of Reformation, Works* (New York, 1936), III, 78–79.

rhetorical methods of the earlier exercises for the poetic looseness of this final form. Other requirements—the ancient descriptions of pastoral peoples, the antiquity of the pastoral as a form
of poetic discourse, the Hebraic parallels, the politico-allegorical
interpretations, the observations of the intenser critics—combined to make this choice certain.

When a Renaissance critic talked about the pastoral, he
frequently recalled that it was at home in Arcadia—where men
were closest to godliness—and referred his readers to the fourth
book of Polybius. When we also turn to this authority so
cherished by seventeenth century republicans, we find ourselves
in an age of gold, among Greek primitives who are not unlike
the citizens of the first garden or those later shepherds whom
the psalmist celebrates. The Arcadians, we are told by Polybius, had a reputation "among all the Greeks for virtue, not
only because of their friendliness to strangers and kindliness in
life and deeds, but above all because of their piety." Besides
these virtues dear to Milton, the Arcadians had a love of
musical harmony which they made the basis of their political
philosophy and the propaedeutic of all education.

> Now it seems to me that the men of old did not introduce
> these things for the sake of luxury or superfluity, but because
> they saw the necessity of personal labor and the painful and
> hard course of their life, and because they consider the aus-
> terity of their manners, which was the consequence of the
> chilly and gloomy climate which prevailed for the most part
> in that region. To our climate all of us become adapted by
> necessity. . . . But the Arcadians, wishing to smooth and
> soften the stubbornness and hardness of nature, introduced
> all the above mentioned things . . . and in short devised all
> manner of measures to tame and soften the hardness of soul
> through education.[18]

This is the testimony of Polybius, and I cannot help but
believe that Milton had read it by 1637.

To this major text must be joined not only the highly

[18] *Op. cit.*, IV, 19–20.

ethical commentary on it written by Guarini in his defense
of pastoral poetry,[19] but also the general attitude of the most
authoritative critics towards the antiquity of the pastoral itself.
It is for them basic pure poetry. Diomedes, Servius, Probus,
and Sabinus, those venerable scholars who congregate in the
dooryard of every Renaissance edition of Vergil, agree that
the pastoral is the most ancient form of poetic expression.
Donatus tells us that Vergil began with the oldest and most
simple form of poetry, passed from this to the middle manner
of the *Georgics*, and thence to the high style of the *Aeneid*.[20]
With this view most Renaissance critics agreed. Puttenham,
the first true English critic, alone took a demurrer, maintaining
that the eclogue was perfected " long after the other *drammatick*
poems " and that its purpose was to " glaunce at greater
matters " " under the vaile of homely persons, and in rude
speeches." [21] In this conclusion Puttenham is an interesting
heretic, whose views were not shared by Rapin [22] nor even by
Fontenelle,[23] who denies that the extant Greek eclogues are
anything like the originals, but who is ready to say that this
mode of poetry is by nature the eldest.

Milton, I expect, would be influenced by the orthodox
attitude; but to the stimulus of writing in the most ancient
of classical manners and in one that was invented by a people
who were intuitively pure in conduct, pious towards the gods,
and democratic in politics should be added the vigorous cogency
of Hebrew pastoralism. It is, perhaps, for this last reason that
metrical paraphrases of the 114th and 118th Psalms are among
Milton's earliest poems. The youthful poet who composed
these metaphrases was certainly aware of the analogue between
the shepherd king of Israel and the pastoral kings of Arcadia
and knew that the relationship between the poetry of the Bible

---

[19] *Compendio della poesia tragicomica* (Bari, 1914), 268–69.

[20] *Vita*, XXII.

[21] *Op. cit.*, 37–38.

[22] *Réflexions sur la poétique* (Paris, 1675), 147–50.

[23] *Poésies Pastorales* (Paris, 1715), 150.

and that of antiquity had been described by every apologist for poets from Boccaccio to Giles Fletcher. The sensitive boy would immediately see the connection between " *Jehova pastor meus est* " and the whole Arcadian tradition, although he would be equally aware that they represented different kinds of outings. It is not impossible that he might identify himself momently with the son of Jesse who calmed the rage of the giant monarch with his inspired harping.

But while he may or may not have been aware of all these inciting traditions, Milton did not overlook, as have many of those who question the ecclesiastical tradition in " Lycidas," the inherited right of the pastoralist to be both satirist and allegorist, to hide, as Puttenham says, something of a topical nature behind the actions and songs of his shepherds. There was, of course, the literary example of Vergil which was modified or dilated by Mantuan, Spenser, and other Renaissance poets. Behind the practice was the agreement of the theoreticians. The grammarians who glossed Vergil were tireless in noticing the historical facts and the political criticism embedded in his *Bucolics*. As a consequence of their observations, the formal critics of the sixteenth century almost recommend this artistic possibility. Pierre de Laudun puts it one way: " Sur les noms de bergers et en leurs devis, bien souvent les bons pöetes y mettent un sens moral et les font parler des affaires d'Etat, des conditions et fortunes des Rois et Princes." [24] William Webbe concurs in this judgment: " For under these personnes, as it were in a cloake of simplicitie, they would eyther set foorth the prayses of theyr freendes, without the note of flattery, or enveigh grievously against abuses, without any token of bytternesse." [25] The pastoral eclogue, it is clear, allowed the poet greater freedom of content than the paramythia. It was a vehicle, then, for a maturer poet.

If the pastoral mode allowed for greater liberty in speaking,

---

[24] *L'art Poétique Français* (Toulouse, 1909), 124.
[25] " A Discourse of English Poetry," in *Elizabethan Critical Eassays* (Oxford, 1904), I, 262.

it also permitted a still greater relaxation in structure. Those modern critics who have complained about the stanzaic and metrical imbalance of " Lycidas " or who have seen it as a series of *canzone* are far, far too modern, for in writing this poem Milton was obeying the kind of literary rule that he liked—the rule that was a rule but at the same time granted freedom. Although he outlines a descriptive formula for the eclogue, Scaliger admits that the pastoral mode is metrically unregulated in half of the known instances. " Sine numero certo, sine lege versus funderent." [26] In his *L'Arte Poetica*, Minturno describes the epicedium as composed of a *propositio* and a *narratio*, with digressions permitted provided that they have some connection with the central proposition.[27] These are the licenses that the critics gave Milton, but if he did not have them, he could have derived them from the etymology of ἐγλογή.

The combined allurements of all these characteristics of pastoral poetry and the fact that epic poets such as Vergil and Spenser often tried their wings on this mode turned Milton towards this form for the last poem of what his generation would have called his melic period. The " Mask " had been pastoral in quality and the same tune is heard faintly in " L'Allegro." We can see that they are all *gradus ad Lycidan*. But the contemporary literary tradition must also not be forgotten, for in " Lycidas " more than in any of the earlier poems its prevalence is manifest.

I have written that the earlier paramythia are mainly exercises based on rhetorical precept and that in the case of the " Fair Infant " the unity rests in the myth; this is not true, to such a large degree, of " Lycidas." Here the response is poetic and it comes as a sensitive re-echoing of ancient elegies as well as those of Petrarch, Boccaccio, Sannazaro, Castiglione, and Spenser. Yet while it is a response, it is also a reaction. It is not a rendering of a classical model; it is not " Galatea,"

---

[26] *Poetices* (1591), 15.   [27] *Op. cit.*, 269–71.

"Ergasto," or "Alcon." It is so totally different from other elegies of the Renaissance and antiquity that were it not for the sheer externalities of the mode, such as the mourning of nature, the summoning of the deities, and the accidental literary recollections [28]—the impedimenta that the glossators have so meticulously recorded—it would hardly seem to belong to the same artistic gender. In the judgment of "Lycidas," as in the judgment of all literature, it is uniqueness that counts; and the secret of "Lycidas" is that though it has universal familiarity, it also has a universal difference. It is this difference that the critics have sensed and tried to understand.

On the surface "Lycidas" is a brilliant poem that captivates our imaginations with the first reading; but when it is placed under the microscope of the critical intelligence, it distresses and disturbs. In the late seventeenth century as in the latter nineteenth century, it was read with admiration, but in the period between, when "decorum" and "propriety" were the critical touchstones, it was found difficult to analyze and estimate. Thyer, whom Newton quotes at the end of his text, noticed a certain "wildness and irregularity" which was both "natural and agreeable" because it fittingly expressed the poet's brief for his friend. To this conclusion Bishop Hurd took exception. The poem, he thought, had an "original air" which did not arise from "any disorder in the plan . . . but in a good degree" from the "looseness and variety of the metre." [29] Johnson, as one might expect, struck with both of his massive fists, for of all critics he alone was unable to see any virtue in "Lycidas."

"Of *Lycidas*, the diction is harsh, the rhymes uncertain, the numbers unpleasing. What beauty there is we must there-

---

[28] The similarities are so frequent that the monody sometimes seems a mosaic of poetic memories: "Who would not sing for Lycidas": "Neget quis carmina Gallo" (Vergil, *Ecl.* 10. 3); "Where were ye nymphs": "πᾶ ποκ' ἄρ' ἦσθ', ὅκα Δάφνις ἐτάκετο, πᾶ ποκα, νύμφαι" (Theocritus, 1. 66); "Phoebus replied and touch'd my trembling ears": "Cynthius aurem vellit et admonuit" (Vergil, *Ecl.* 6. 3).

[29] Milton, *Works* (ed. Todd, London, 1852), III, 370.

fore seek in the sentiments and images." It has no real passion; " where there is leisure for fiction there is little grief." When he considers the " sentiments " and the " images," he finds them trite, insincere, " disgusting." The poet, moreover, mingles " the most awful and sacred truths" with trifling fictions. " Lycidas " is not even damned with faint praise. To Johnson's aspersions, Thomas Warton, as was his custom, offered a disclaimer, for he lacked both Johnson's prejudices and sharpness of observation. His defense is best described by his last statement: " These irregularities and incongruities cannot be tried by modern criticism." To be sure, the poem is filled with trite expressions; to be sure, the pastoral form is disgusting; but these qualities are characteristic of the seventeenth century. " Our poetry was not yet purged of its Gothick combinations." If it has no passion, let us read it for its poetry.[30]

The nineteenth century, when it thought of " Lycidas," tried a different tack. Hallam remarks that his predecessors, and especially Johnson, judged the poem by the too narrow standards of the narrative or the dramatic poem. Poems of this type " pretend to no credibility, they aim at no illusion; they are read with the willing abandonment of the imagination to a waking dream, and require only that general possibility, that combination of images which common experience does not reject as incompatible." [31] Hazlitt's defense of " Lycidas " is at the same time a romantic peroration and an onslaught on Johnson's objection to the classical echoes in the poem. " They convey," Hazlitt writes, " a positive identity beyond the mere name. We refer them to something out of ourselves. It is only by an effort of abstraction that we divest ourselves of the idea of their reality." [32] Tennyson was content simply to echo Warton and call the poem " a touchstone of poetic taste." In other words, the nineteenth century attempts to avoid the criticism of the eighteenth century, of Johnson really, by vague-

[30] *Poems upon Several Occasions* (London, 1791), 35–37.
[31] *Introduction to the Literature of Europe* (New York, 1880), III, 261.
[32] *Complete Works* (London, 1930), IV, 31–36.

ness. Both attitudes, I think, show an unreadiness to come to grips with the poem.

Legouis put his finger on the central problem when he wrote: " Ce n'est pas King qu'il faut y chercher, c'est Milton lui-meme." [33] No one had ever asked who the true subject of the elegy was, and when Legouis made this statement, he introduced a just speculation that brings us far closer to the meaning and the passion of this poem than ever we were before. Seizing on this hint, Tillyard went on to explicate the poem and to give it a new cohesion by demonstrating its basic egocentricity.[34] Daiches, the most recent explicator, broadens the theme: " It is man in his creative capacity, man in his capacity for achieving something significant in his span on earth, man as a Christian humanist." [35] Both of these critics are correct, but neither is correct by himself. As all of Milton's successful poems, " Lycidas " moves as a pendulum between the universal and the particular, between the special lesson of the inner Milton and the cosmic principle drawn therefrom that each man is part of the human estate. The subject of the poem is seldom Edward King, and his death is not the real occasion of the poem. The eighteenth century thought it was; hence they missed the central passion and the gnawing grief.

The old techniques of the paramythia are at once suggested and avoided. There is a hint of a φύσις and a παιδεία, but they are lacking in the particular attributes of a personal intent. The drowned shepherd was a poet and the companion of the celebrator; together they watched their flocks, together they played their flutes to win the approval of the old singing master Damoetas. There is no special identification in this. The customary consolatio is properly at the end, and though it is more than an ordinary marriage of Christian and pagan memories, it is not a marriage of convenience. Lycidas does not become a star, though the metamorphosis is implicit in the

---

[33] *Histoire de la Littérature Anglaise* (Paris, 1933), 567.
[34] *Milton* (London, 1930), 80–85.
[35] *A Study of Literature* (Ithaca, New York, 1948), 173.

concluding imagery, for his spiritual transformation exceeds this. As a Christian saint he becomes a measure in the heavenly song, but as an Arcadian shepherd he remains the guardian genius of the western shore. Milton elaborates in this way his earlier statements about the omnipresence of the great dead, but he maintains a distinction between the manifestations of this presence in classical and Christian terms.

Though the poem is about Milton and the question that lies on the top of his mind, a mythic identification is invented, as in his first English elegy, and pervades the whole of " Lycidas."

> What could the Muse herself that *Orpheus* bore,
> The Muse herself, for her enchanting son
> Whom Universal nature did lament,
> When by the rout that made the hideous roar,
> His gory visage down the stream was sent,
> Down the swift *Hebrus* to the *Lesbian* shore?

Orpheus dead is for Milton an inescapable myth. It found its way into " L'Allegro " and " Il Penseroso " where it symbolizes and unifies; it will be renewed in the solemn invocation to the seventh book of *Paradise Lost*. The Elizabethans were infatuated with the legend of the master of the seven-stringed lyre and the lyric harrower of Hell; [36] Milton, though he is most aware of Orpheus' place in the history of harmony, chooses with exquisite care the last somber event as an ænigmatic reminder. In one way the death of Orpheus is the death of King: " Whilst thee the shores, and sounding Seas/Wash far away, where'er thy bones are hurl'd."

But there is more to it than this. Orpheus, the poet divinely instructed by Apollo and the Muses, Orpheus the assailer of rudeness and irreligion, and Orpheus, the priest whose almost Christian dogma is summarized by Suidas [37] and thence tran-

---

[36] J. Wirl, " Orpheus in der englischen Literatur," *Wiener Beiträge zur Englischen Philologie*, XL (1913), 1–66; Miss Mayerson has treated this problem in a somewhat different way in *PMLA*, LXIV (1949), 189–207.

[37] *Historica* (Basel, 1564), 703.

scribed by scholars of the Renaissance,[38] becomes the center of the symbolic narrative. The theme that evolves is that of resurrection, and the implications of the theme are obvious even though there was no fact to bolster them. The veil is really thin, for Milton could not have been ignorant of Celsus' contention that Orpheus was a nobler saviour than Christ.[39] It is a sort of analogy that Milton found unavoidable: Christ-Orpheus-Milton; just as later he will think in terms of Samson-Hercules-Milton.

The governing symbolic narrative which allows " Lycidas " to be translated into three inner languages is in part an expansion of the method of the first English elegy, where the supporting myths were not only multiple but had no immediate purpose beyond ornamentation and associative continuity. Thanks to the critical tradition of the Arcadian elegy, the structure of " Lycidas " is more relaxed, and it is this relaxation that gives it its exceeding power. Miltonists have too often overlooked the new freedom that is plain in this poem because they have sought for the familiar, for the time-chewed analogues; hence when they have looked at " Lycidas " as a whole, some of them have seen it only as a hodge-podge of literary fragments assembled contrary to the usual elegiac order and disturbed by the *intruding* digressions on the fate of the poet and the prospects of the priest. Some of them have apologized for Milton by suggesting that Pindar was his guide or by informing us that though he misunderstood what he was about, his intent was sincere.

Yet it is these so-called digressions that give the poem its true form by coinciding with the triple myth. They marshal the conventions of the pastoral eclogue into something totally new. The poem faces the fact of death squarely, but in doing so, it asks three questions that have troubled the poet for a long time. His previous poems of this sort had been purely descriptive and had followed some aspect of the old rhetorical

[38] See Gyraldus, *Syntagma Deorum, Opera* (Leyden, 1696), I, 413.
[39] Origen, *Contra Celsum, PG,* XI, 1498.

formula, although they had often terminated in a Christian stratagem. Here the poet has it out with God. On one side of the tribunal is Milton, the poet and possible candidate for priesthood, who is only too well aware of the fragility and eccentricities of Providence. On the other side is Milton, the instrument of God and the possessor of the " prophetic strain," who is eager to explain to himself and to all men the inscrutable plans of the unknowable. In every respect, I think, " Lycidas " is his first attempt to "assert eternal Providence and justify the ways of God to men." The poem, then, actually consists of three parts and the major divisions come at " Of so much fame in Heav'n " (84) and " Stands ready to smite once " (131). In each of the poetic sections preceding the divisions, a question is asked and triumphantly answered in a great vocal crescendo. In the last part the particular questions of the first two sections are raised to the universal; and when the ultimate answer comes, it comes with an actuality of conviction that has never been attained by any other English poet.[40]

The poem begins with slow reluctance. Once more the poet, hesitant in performance because of his conscious poetical unripeness, has been summoned to lament the death of a friend. He pretends that the poem is squeezed out of him and the words that he uses—*forced, shatter, compels, constraint*—make strong the sense of his own unreadiness. The " mellowing year " has come neither to him nor to the botanical symbols of his craft; hence the season of fruitage is anticipated as with " rude fingers " he plucks the green berries of the laurel, myrtle, and ivy. But a poet is dead—a poet as unripe as he. Does God give men talents to use in his service only to let them be wasted? Is Providence justified in this? In a way, it is Milton whom Milton mourns, but it is not a selfish type of mourning. It is not the mourning of a man frightened by his own eventual death but that of one who is confused, who has been given a task by God but perhaps not the time in which to complete it.

[40] A. Barker, " The Pattern of Milton's *Nativity Ode*," *University of Toronto Quarterly*, X (1941), 171–72, furnished me with this suggestion.

It is a theme central to the two great sonnets. It is also the first question that must be answered.

The ornamental expressions that preside over the first part of the poem are all half-familiar, but when we inspect them closely, we discover that the governing metaphors are floral. The classical hyacinth and rose of the earlier epicedium have become a great garden, but it is not a garden to gladden the severe English eye. The garden is unwatered and disordered. The adjectives are dismal: *brown, sere, harsh, crude, rude, bitter, sad, parching, sable, heavy, desert, wild, remorseless, hideous, gory.* The thyme is wild, the vine gadding and o'ergrown, the top of Mona is shaggy. Living color is almost wanting. The green of the hazels and the willows is only a remembrance. Alone in this autumnal garden the white thorn blooms unseasonably, showing the mourning color, or rather absence of color, for those who die too young. The dreariness that precedes the first question is increased by sickness brought to flowers and beasts by the canker, the frost, and the taint-worm. Then death, who is also in Arcady—*Et in Arcadia ego*—comes. The druid bards, who preserved according to seventeenth century thinking the ancient Orphic rites, are all dead, and the torn body of Orpheus himself floats "down the swift Hebrus to the Lesbian shore." This is all preparation to what has been called the first digression. The approach has been gradual: plants, animals, the demigod. With Milton we have ascended the ladder of being in a depressing waste.[41]

The poet asks the question that is at once subjective and universal. It is a poet's question, but it is also the question of a poet who is a metaphysician. The first half of the question was formerly posited in *Comus* so to some degree we already know the answer. The sensuous world lies before us; it is what we know. But the mind, prompted by an involuntary

[41] Since I read this paper in 1950 to the Johns Hopkins Philological Association, I have been anticipated here in print by a far better analysis; see W. Shumaker, "Flowerets and Sounding Seas," *PMLA*, LXVI (1951), 485–94.

mechanism, strains beyond this. It denies the senses to learn that which is only partially knowable but eminently convincing. For men of Milton's persuasion this yearning for supra-sensual ends was one of the proofs of the immortality of the soul; it was the way to the " prophetic strain." For the " strong spirits " of that generation it was the limit of folly. This is one of the central problems of *Comus* and Milton now returns to it. What is the poet's guerdon? Are they not wiser—poets like Catullus and Johannes Secundus—who sport with Amaryllis in the shade than those who refine their poetic gifts and employ them as perfect instruments in the praise of God? " Fame," says the Renaissance, " is the spur," but Milton had long before found a higher definition of this word.

> We living mortals particularly are to be cheated out of glory, while a long chain and descent of years has made famous those illustrious ancients; we, in the decadent old age of the world, we, by the speedy destruction of all things, are to be overwhelmed, if we shall have left behind anything to be extolled with everlasting praise; our name is to abide but a short time, for hardly may any posterity succeed to its memory; vain is it now to produce so many books and eminent monuments of ability, which the approaching funeral pyre of the world will consume. I do not deny that this can very likely take place. But, in truth, not to value fame when you have done well, that is beyond all glory. How little has the idle discourse of men enriched the departed and the dead, discourse of which no delight, no emotion could reach them? May we hope for an eternal life, which will never wipe out the memory at least of our good deeds on earth; in which, if we have nobly deserved anything here, we ourselves, being present shall hear it.[42]

There is, then, a Parnassus of Permanence in Heaven where God, who is the greatest of literary critics, makes all the final decisions. We are not surprised to discover that Fame—not the multitongued Rumor of earth—sits at the feet of God and

[42] *Seventh Prolusion, Works* (New York, 1931), XII, 278-80.

proclaims the loyalty of Abdiel, the dreadless angel, far faster than a seraph can fly. The first question is answered. He who loses his fame shall find it. But there is a second question, for which a poetic preparation is necessary.

The dominant metaphors of the first preparation are floral. They were sometimes poet's flowers, blossoms of fame, but they partly reveal in their unripe yet wintered aspects the whispered pledge of resurrection. The metaphors of the second preparation are all based on water and in this there is a triple implication. The poet had been drowned and Cambridge lies in a watery land; then, too, for Milton's readers water was a symbol of terrestrial and eternal life. Orpheus had been flung in the stream, but his disciple Heraclitus had said that to souls " it is death to become water, and to water it is death to become earth, but from earth comes water, and from water soul." [43] It was by no accident that the ancients pretended that Venus, the magna mater, had been born of the froth of the sea; the Renaissance had this legend by heart. It is unnecessary, I expect, to make the Christian transference and to expatiate on the waters of life. Milton implies this by stating the pagan alternatives, adorning the universal symbol with narrative figments such as the Sicilian Arethusa, the Vergilian Mincius, Triton, Hippotades, the inventor of winglike sails. As the flowers of the first passage are colorless, the waters of the second passage are stagnant. There is an oily description of the level brine, so calm that " sleek Panope " could sport on it with all her sisters. The Mincius is " smooth-sliding," the Irish Sea is airless, the reed-choked Cam comes " footing slow." The waters are either becalmed, motionless, or, at best, hardly perceptible in motion; for as the flowers of the first part are dry, the waters of the second part are unliving. The principal adjectives are again of a distressing nature: *felon, hard, rugged, beaked, fatal,*

[43] Clemens, *Stromatum*, VI, 16, quoted in Diels, *Die Fragmente der Vorsokratiker* (Berlin, 1912), I, 85. This subject has been treated at length by R. P. Adams, " Death and Rebirth in ' Lycidas '," *PMLA*, LXIV (1949), 183–88.

perfidious, dark. We appoach the second question through a cumulative metaphor—that of a dying world presided over by birds of prey.

The second question is parallel to the first in that it again interrogates the Providence of God. Orpheus, as Lycidas, had been both pastoral priest and poet and we know that Milton himself had only recently decided against taking holy orders. The question may betray his true reason for his decision. The church is corrupt. " The hungry sheep look up and are not fed." The preying wolf battens on the flock. Is Providence wise? In permitting the death of Lycidas and others devoted as he, God seems to have squandered idly one of his truest servants. Once more the answer is based on faith rather than on logic, for logic, as any poet knows, is no child of the Logos. God will see that his ends are reached. The church has lived through the generations though men have served it badly; it is itself, as its apologists said, the proof of its own divine ordination. The two-handed engine which carries the double death of body and soul, the *gladius Dei* of iron and gold that twice damns the atheist priest, will avenge St. Peter's wrongs. " God does not need," Milton will say later, " either man's work or his deeds."

The two questions on which the whole structure of this poem turns are answered in terms of man's acceptance of God's will. Philosophy, as it does in all of Milton's poetry, bows to theology; with this gesture one moves from the homocentric to the theocentric world and all things change. The fact of death becomes truly unimportant and the world which had been dead, dry, colorless, and stagnant comes bursting into life. In similar wise, the waters of life, which had rotted or lain almost without motion, race in their currents and thunder in their roaring. The flowers flash into brightness and order; the ground, as at Creation, is green and purple; the " well attir'd Woodbine " supplants the " gadding vine." Brooks gush; Alpheus spreads his streams; the sea sounds and washes round the world. All is color and motion as the brooding melancholy of the poet is swept away by his angelic understanding of the ultimate solution of what he had formerly seen as poignant aspects of the problem of evil, of the unintelligibility of Providence. The poem now swirls towards a mystical conclusion and we leave the particular earthly anxieties of the poet and priest to enjoy the harmonic beatitude reserved for all Christian men. All Heaven comes before our eyes.

Through the deep reaches of the kingdom of sea beasts, "the monstrous world," the vast oceanic currents bear the mortal remains of Lycidas. That which seemed to be life has returned to the source of seeming life. But the *anima*, which has descended from the breath breathed in Adam's nostrils, has risen above the realm of earth and water, above the kingdom of air and fire. It cannot become a star because it has ascended above the sphere of stars.

> So *Lycidas*, sunk low, but mounted high,
> Through the dear might of him that walk'd the waves,
> Where other groves, and other streams along,
> With *Nectar* pure his oozy Locks he laves,
> And hears the unexpressive nuptial Song,
> In the blest Kingdoms meek of joy and love.
> There entertain him all the Saints above,
> In solemn troops, and sweet Societies
> That sing, and singing in their glory move,
> And wipe the tears for ever from his eyes.

Paul Elmer More once wrote that in these ten lines Milton expressed more exquisitely than any other poet the Christian answer to the fact of death and that he achieved this by means of nothing but commonplace turns of phrase.[44] There is no reason for pause over this fact, for there is no other way to describe Heaven save in trite phrases from the Bible and the Book of Common Prayer. This is the Christian alphabet by which all is spelled; to use other letters is to impoverish the imagination.

By the clear and fresh ordering of Christian clichés, Milton

[44] "How to Read *Lycidas*," *The Amercian Review*, VII (1936), 140–58.

answers the universal question that is the pre-text of " Lycidas."
With it are answered the special questions of the poet-priest.
About this question the thread of the elegy is wound so that
its very weaknesses, as they have been called, give the poem
strength and power. The question is answered with a timeless
and universal authority, and though other poets will rephrase
it, all their answers are but echoes of this. We can see, too,
that the sections that have been admired because they can be
glossed are merely ancillary; through them the reader is led
to what is new and important. But there is also a kind of
epilogue.

The celebrant poet, having sung his new song, wraps his
cloak about him and departs. " To-morrow to fresh Woods,
and Pastures new." We are told that this is a conventional
conclusion or that it refers to the projected Italian journey.
This may well be true, but the poem, we remember, began
with reluctance, the hesitation of a man who like one of the
great prophets felt as yet unready for his predetermined task.
The predestined work for which God had fitted him required
a seemingly endless preparation before it could be begun; yet
somewhere along the way stood the menacing shadow of meager
death, the threatening, horrible interrupter. But the fear is
gone now, purgation of doubts is certain and has come with
the completion of the elegy. Milton upheld by the arms of
Providence has stared Death down. The melic period is ended;
there is renewed confidence for the greater task.

IV

THE IDEA AS PATTERN:

Despair and "Samson Agonistes"

*M*ILTON, like all other good men, has a precise understanding of the ingenerate pathos of evil, a pathos that
manifests itself most poignantly in the continual tawdry imitation of the good. The Satan of *Paradise Lost* has no conception
of God's real spiritual essence or divine attributes. As the
shallow-minded, he understands only externals; hence, he is
forever imitating the material evidence of God's power and
glory. His imitations are so cheap, so flimsy and fearfully
unoriginal that only those who are already drunk with sin or
those in whom evil is in a state of becoming fail to discern the
incredible cheat. So Milton sees to it that the fallen angels
erect among the dust and cinders of Hell a towered city not
unlike the one that God created for the saints, and he describes
the demonic civility as if it were a distorted reflection of that
of Heaven.[1] There is something ludicrously claptrap and subur-
ban about the whole hellish enterprise, and this for Milton and
for his contemporary readers was shockingly amusing.

The modern readers of *Paradise Lost*, like the enticed sons

[1] This notion is continuously brought out and it begins before Satan's
fall. The "Palace of great *Lucifer*" was "In imitation of that Mount
whereon/*Messiah* was declar'd" and here is "pretending" and "counter-
feited truth" (V. 764–66). Mammon in his oration sees opportunities
to imitate Heaven in Hell (II. 262–73); at the dissolution of the Stygian
Council, Satan appears surrounded by a globe of fiery seraphim "with
pomp Supreme,/And God-like imitated State" (II. 506–13). Whenever
Satan affects any goodness, like the Sodom apples, it is always spurious.

of Seth, have descended to the plains of reason and made a troth with the fry of demons; hence, they fail to perceive the tilt of the jest and make greater the laughter of the citizens of the Miltonic paradise. They see in Satan a kind of tragic king, not too different from those fated heroes of the Greek tragedians except that he expresses himself, as all the other characters of *Paradise Lost*, in the purest form of the Hebrew tongue. They do this because they forget that one of the satiric methods of this earlier generation was to exalt the object of derision before it was shaken apart by hard mockery. And so unless we think of Satan as a fitting antagonist for Eve, he is no hero; in fact, in all his Miltonic entrances, he is everything but that. His weaknesses of mind and heart are consistently displayed as he flees before the flashing laughter of the saints ascended and ascendant as a lone man before a rage of arrows.

Twice in the course of *Paradise Lost* wry laughter is heard as Satan, in self-assumed exaltation, imitates the imperial manner of God. Once it is explicit in the hisses of his barons as he reports his sad success against the father and mother of men; and once it is implicit in the description of the shoddy monarch on his glittering throne of royal state.

> And from despair
> Thus high uplifted beyond hope, aspires
> Beyond thus high, insatiate to pursue
> Vain War with Heav'n (II. 6–9).

The humor, as I see it, is in the word *despair*, for despair is the passionate quality of the defeated Satan and we must often substitute it for the governing passion of pride which had fathered his defeat. Pride expounds the fall in Heaven, despair is the pervading and motivating emotion of him who is Hell;

> And in the lowest deep a lower deep
> Still threat'ning to devour me opens wide,
> To which the Hell I suffer seems a Heav'n
> (IV. 76–78).

Despair, which is the passion farthest from the love of God, precipitates him from deep to unfathomable deep. " Farthest from Him is best." But unrelieved despair without the meed of rational or spiritual hope is hardly the conventional endowment of a hero.

It is not unfitting that desperation should be the guiding Satanic passion, for Satan is the master sinner and so he must be the master of the three greatest sins: unbelief, hatred of God, and despair. At one time or other, he is the poetic exemplar of this frightening triplicity of evil, but since despair is the one sin most likely to infect the sons of Adam, Milton expounds it most zealously. Satan's pride is sickened by despair on the third day of the war in Heaven when he sees the chariot of God's Son, flashing with eyes and wings, advance against his terrified ranks.

> This saw his hapless Foes, but stood obdur'd,
> And to rebellious fight rallied thir Powers
> Insensate, hope conceiving from despair
>
> (VI. 785–87) .

Milton knew that despair is the hidden but false lining of the cloak of pride, because, as pride, it is gestated in the minds of those who are farthest from God. He knew, as Burton knew,[2] that despair on a human level sometimes attends the achievement of the impossible. " Nec alia causa victoriae quam quod desperaverant." Satan, whose human reactions are witnesses to his ungodliness, is possessed of this sort of despair as Christ's enormous engine scatters his bruised battalions. It is certainly this " hope beyond despair " that plagues him during the whole course of the first of the " grand consults," just as it is the dominating emotion of the last consult in *Paradise Regained*. But we should not be misled by our human appraisal of desperate courage; what we may admire in a man is not necessarily admirable in an archangel, fallen though he may be. This

---

[2] *Anatomy of Melancholy* (ed. Shilleto, London, 1893), III, 449–52.

apparent virtue, like the palaces of Hell, is a total sham, for against God there is no hope of victory.

Though despair may sometimes produce a kind of courage in Satan, it is oftener an infertile quality. Milton frequently informs us that the inner heart of Satan is rotten with desperation. When, during the consultation with Beelzebub—a consultation in commemoration of an earlier one in the northern or rebellious shires of Heaven—Satan boasts of his military advantages, Milton hastens to expose this brag as one that has no prop other than inward despair (I. 126). On the same occasion Satan argues that despair will beget resolution (I. 188–91), but he controverts his own feeble conclusion by concealing his tearing desperation from his reviving paladins (I. 522–25). God comments on Satan's plans for a " desperate revenge " (III. 85), but Milton lets us count the lines that despair has written in Satan's faded cheeks. There is more than this, for the pain of this increasing illness distorts all of Satan's judgments. The beauty of flowered Eden charms even the messengers from Paradise, yet it is only a partial anodyne for Satan, banishing " all saddness but despair " (IV. 155–56), the slumbering despair that had shortly before been awakened by the sight of the flaming ministry of the sun (IV. 23–24). We know exactly how the mental processes of the tarnished angel turn: " Me miserable! which way shall I fly/ Infinite wrath and infinite despair? " (IV. 73–74).

Despair and wrath—these are the two grinding stones between which Satan is eternally milled. Pride which invests Satan with all that is humanly best is ironically enough followed by inevitable despair which strips all dignity from him. In a psychological sense Satan's tragedy is his constant loss of dignity: first, a battered archangel, then a super-subtle politician, a spy and pryer, a tiger, a cormorant, a toad, a snake. He comes a long journey down the road of being and at each milestone his dignity dwindles. Yet the declination of his self-esteem arms him with a new weapon; it teaches him to destroy the dignity of others. Each of his temptations—that of the hosts in Heaven, that of Sin, and that of Eve—has this exquisite conclusion, and, as time passes, it becomes his most demonic device.

The desperation that is incarnate in Satan, that governs so many of his actions and modulates so many of his decisions is shared by his companions in sin. Moloch, who has been taught despair at the hands of Gabriel, bases his advice for the continuation of the war on this principle alone. From Dante and from Spenser we learn, if we only take tuition from poets, that despair may drive one into the unforgivable sin of suicide, and so Moloch, " now fiercer by despair " (II. 45), urges a suicidal assault on the wakeful citadels of Heaven.

> More destroy'd than thus
> We should be quite abolisht and expire   (II. 92–93).

This is the Judas-consequence of the betrayal of God, and it suggests to the sophist Belial and the empire-builder Mammon a solution most contrary. Moloch, says Belial, " grounds his courage on despair " (II. 126), a despair without hope.

> Thus repuls'd, our final hope
> Is flat despair   (II. 142–143).

Then Mammon, we recall, supports the contention of Belial with practical observations on the natural resources of Hell, and for a moment the demons almost vote lack of confidence in the prime minister. Yet there is irony here and the clear laughter of God is heard again. Whereas Moloch's despair and his suicidal intents provide Belial with a witty enthymeme, Belial and his companions are no less desperate themselves.

Everyone has observed that Belial is the incarnation of sloth (" Belial came last ") and Mammon the personification of materialism (" admiring more/the riches of Heav'n's pavements, trodd'n gold "), but no one seems ever to have wondered why a totally lazy man or an aurophile would join the ranks of a revolutionary army. We can understand, I imagine, why Moloch or Arioch or Asmadai are with the rebels, but revolutions, as history tells us, seldom attract slothful men or banking magnates. Viewed in the light of historical biography, Belial and Mammon seem more like the supporters of reaction or at least of the status quo; yet somehow or other they have been seduced by the banners of revolt. There is, of course, some justification in regarding the civil war provoked by Satan as a war of reaction. The politics of Heaven have been radically altered as far as the limited intelligence of the bitter general can understand. In a sense Satan yearns for "the good old days" of individual enterprise. But we had best turn to theology for its wisdom.

Despair, writes St. Paschasius, springs from sloth, from a love of temporal possessions, from monstrous desires, and from prideful contempt. With these phrases he blankets all the demons of *Paradise Lost*, but he adds that sloth is the most common source of despair since it whispers that the precepts of God are impossible, "so the soul is put to sleep and oppressed with such languor that it does not wish to awaken." [3] The seemingly particular emphasis on sloth is really not unusual—most theologians describe despair as one of the six branches of *acedia* or *tristitia*—and this association is illustrated by Augustine's account of the inward conversation of the despairing soul. "Now I have sinned; now I am damned; God will not overlook such sins; why not add sin to sins? I shall enjoy my life with pleasure, lasciviousness, and wicked desire. Now that I have lost hope of redemption, I shall have what I know, if I cannot have what I believe." [4] St. Thomas, as was his custom, simplified this discussion by stating that despair arises either from sloth or lust. The former vice leads one to believe that good is unachievable, the latter convinces one that it is not to be desired. [5]

Though their despair is unacknowledged, Belial and Mam-

---

[3] *De Fide, PL,* CXX. 1450–55.

[4] *Enarratio in Psalmum L, PL,* XXXVI, 588.

[5] *Summa Theologica,* II. 2. 20. See also Suarez, *Opera omnia* (Paris, 1856), IV, 468; Zanchius, *Opera* (1605), IV, 292–94. The same opinions are shared by both protestants and Romans.

mon are as desperate as Moloch; they have simply not arrived at the ridiculous end of self-destruction that Moloch sees as a grateful alternative to victory. And it may be added that they know it is impossible to reach this end without the help of him with whom they contend. " Whether our angry Foe/Can give it, or will ever? " Yet the germ of desperation fattens in them. Mammon is besotted with a love of temporal possessions; Belial is a slothful and lecherous devil.

> Thou thyself doat'st on womankind, admiring
> Thir shape, thir colour, and attractive grace, . . .
> Cast wanton eyes on the daughters of men,
> And coupl'd with them, and begot a race
>
> (*PR*, II. 175–76, 180–81) .

The two demons may be revolutionaries because this is a reactionary uprising and they are really reactionaries. They may also be on this side because they are exemplifications of deadly sins and because they are, as a result, desperate of good. This distance from the will of God is damnation.

The despair of demons is a special study in itself and it is something totally impossible for even the most gifted of metaphysicians to analyze. Despair, too, as Dante instructs us, is the pervading mood of all those lost souls who dwell in Hell, and Milton does not delay to tell us why demons are doubly desperate.

> The first sort by thir own suggestion fell,
> Self-tempted, self-deprav'd: Man falls deceiv'd
> By the other first: Man therefore shall find grace,
> The other none   (III. 129–32) .

These are God's words and with them grace and mercy, those alleviators of mortal guiltiness, are wiped forever from the sight of demons. The edict of Heaven makes laughable those occasional moments of self-interrogation concerning forgiveness that one finds in Satan's autobiography. Despair is as proper to Hell as black fire, but living men can circumvent this evil. Even Judas and Cain, whom Milton mentions in his account of despair,[6] were not in their life-times beyond the limits of grace, and it is with the living, not with those desperadoes of eternity, that Milton is concerned. It is they whom Milton would rescue, for, as the theologians inform us, there is no salvation for them who die in despair. Hence, if the reader is to be here taught a Christian lesson, Milton must translate the matter into human symbols. This he does in the story of Adam and Eve.

Unlike most of his children, Adam has intelligential lessonings that enable him to understand abstruse matters without the necessity of experience. He knows by nature that Satan is a desperate creature and describes him as such when he informs Eve of the possibility of temptation.

> Envying our happiness, and of his own
> Despairing, seeks to work us woe and shame
> By sly assault   (IX. 254–56) .

Envy and despair are the main supports of Satan's temptation; so it should not astonish us that the immediate result of the fall of Adam and Eve is despair itself.

> Love was not in thir looks, either to God
> Or to each other, but apparent guilt,
> And shame, and perturbation, and despair
>
> (X. 111–13) .

In time a partly convalesced Adam will inform the archangel Michael that despair is one of the intellectual burdens that has been his since the Fall (XI. 301) , but an important moral history precedes this confession.

After the eating of the forbidden apple and its immediate sinful consequences, Adam endures a wasted night in Eden that is an artistic contrast to the placid and ideally happy evening that Milton described with so much Christian pleasure in the fourth book of the epic. The lamentation of the father

---

[6] *De doctrina Christiana, Works* (New York, 1931) , XVII, 56–58.

of men, no longer erect but prostrate on the chilly floor of the
garden, is a kind of bitter Christian echo to the sleepless nights
and amorous complaints of the " starved Lover " of the Pe-
trarchean tradition. Remorse, despair, and self-accusation make
hideous the loneliness of the uxorious Adam. For once he lies
alone; for once he does not sleep. Suicide is not in his mind,
but the death-wish is. *Tristitia* has bound him.

> O welcome hour whenever! why delays
> His hand to execute what his Decree
> Fix'd on this day? why do I overlive,
> Why am I mockt with death, and length'n'd out
> To deathless pain? how gladly would I meet
> Mortality my sentence, and be Earth
> Insensible, how glad would lay me down
> As in my Mother's lap?   (X. 771–78) .

As his descendant Job, Adam momently shuns in his heart the
will of God although the thought of avoiding it is never his.
" Curse God," says Job's wife in the protestant text, " and die,"
but Job knows better than she, and with extraordinary patience,
he awaits the unfolding of the divine plan. Eve is the true
ancestress of Job's wife.

Theology, which was far more experienced than Adam
although he was regarded by the seventeenth century as the
primate of theologians, knew that the monster promoters of
Christian despair were an overwhelming sense of sin and a mis-
conception of the all-embracing mercy of God, a mercy that
was part of his love for his creatures. Adam, made ignorant
by sin, shows his black blindness of this when he says:

> as my Will
> Concurr'd not to my being, it were but right
> And equal to reduce me to my dust,
> Desirous to resign, and render back
> All I receiv'd, unable to perform
> Thy terms too hard, by which I was to hold
> The good I sought not (X. 746–52) .

The truth is that Adam and Eve (he with his curiosity and uxoriousness, she with her pride and inward rebellion) fell steadily from the day of their creation and are finally made aware of the fall through the symbolic disobedience of taste; hence, they now misunderstand God's mercy as before they misunderstood his will. For them the requirements of God's will are too difficult, so they excuse themselves by insisting that the will of man is too weak. " Now I have sinned, now I am damned." The only release from this unequal contest between the infinite and the finite that they can understand is death. This is, according to the theologians, the traditional illogical course of men who reason without faith in the infinite mercy of God. By this infinity all finiteness is erased. We remember, of course, the argument that Despair puts in the head of the Red Cross Knight who, ignorant of God's mercy, drinks in the seemingly rational discourse of the frightening personification and is only saved from self-destruction by the dogmatic action of Christian Truth.[7] It is a similar conclusion that the grasping but spiritually naive mind of Faustus reaches.

> *Stipendium peccati mors est.* Ha! *Stipendium.* . . The reward of sin is death: that's hard. *Si peccasse negamus, fallimur, et nulla est in nobis veritas.* If we say that we have no sin, we deceive ourselves, and there's no truth in us. Why, then belike, we must sin, and so consequently die.
> Ay, we must die an everlasting death.[8]

The death-wish of Adam stems from a feeling of helplessness and emptiness of soul that is similar to that of the Red Cross Knight and of the Faustus of the latter scenes. But Adam is recreated by her whom he regards as his destroyer, for Milton puts into the mind of Eve the only two possible cures for the wounds of despair. The summit of desperation that Adam has climbed is like the pinnacle of the temple, a point of uneasy equilibrium; one must either stand through divine ministration or fall to perdition. By some sort of hazy intuition, Eve seems

---

[7] *Faerie Queene,* I. ix. 38–47.   [8] *Doctor Faustus,* I. i. 39–44.

to know this. Without quite understanding the true nature of her suggestion, she proposes the first Christian cure.

> And to the place of judgment will return,
> There with my cries importune Heaven, that all
> The sentence from thy head remov'd may light
> On me (X. 932–35) .

With this self-effacing suggestion Eve sows the seed of regeneration, but being of a simpler spiritual constitution than her mate, she almost sows it in thorny ground; for shortly thereafter, she thinks of the other way, the way of damnation.

> Let us seek Death, or he not found, supply
> With our own hands his Office on ourselves;
> Why stand we longer shivering under fears,
> That show no end but Death, and have the power,
> Of many ways to die the shortest choosing,
> Destruction with destruction to destroy (X. 1001–1006) .

It is this proposal that brings about the spiritual rally in Adam as he rejects it together with Eve's other suggestion of a fruitless marriage. Both are frantic escapes from reality—if reality may be thought of as the will of God—yet they trouble the stagnant pool of Adam's memory and he finally recalls the affectionate mercy of the celestial judge who pronounced their penalties. So the seed of Eve's earlier suggestion is warmed by the recollection and its flower is prayer, the most certain symbol of divine mercy. The mere proposal vanquishes despair.

I expect that Milton saw in the fable that he invented for the tenth book a kind of moral narrative. Despair, sprouting from sin and from a sense of unworthiness or from an unknowingness of mercy, is for corporeal man supreme disobedience to the will of God. If he continues in this state of spiritual sloth, the mind of man will turn to the death-hunger which may propel him, as Saul was propelled, into damnation as complete and eternal as that of the demons. The soul cure is simple. Patiently and obediently man must await the revelation of God's will supported by an extraordinary confidence in divine love and mercy. Adam comes eventually to this conclusion and he is rewarded with a prophetic vision that makes patience easier and obedience more sure. But Milton is never content to make a point once or to make it in a subordinate fashion; he elaborates this theme in *Samson Agonistes*, which is his proudest analysis of the problem of Christian despair. I shall begin my explication by discarding.

First, I am sure that Milton's self-identification with the young judge of Israel did much to raise the character of that primitive ruffian of a half-savage legend to nobler heights than the compilers of the Book of Judges could possibly imagine. The hairy sun symbol of the oldest of Jewish myths, who seems so repulsive to those who do not read his story with sanctified inattention, becomes in the great tragic poem a mighty Christian hero, worthy of all those prophetic embellishments with which a thousand years of Christian exegesis had adorned him. Yet the whole intent of the tragedy has been somewhat obscured by some scholars who are more interested in autobiography than in poetry. Certainly Milton was blind, certainly he thought of himself as God's champion among a faithless people, but to say this is merely to conclude that he found the legend of Samson a congenial subject. This is possibly the first rule of artistic effort, but not its end.

In general the slight critical literature on this poem centers about the alterations in the protagonist's character as a species of continual rebuke to Johnson's complaint that " the intermediate parts have neither cause nor consequence, neither hasten nor retard the catastrophe." I should like to join this movement, but I cannot promise to keep step. By carefully describing Samson's slow-witted realization of the fact that he is God's man against the Philistine's Dagon, critics have revealed a dramatic pattern that Johnson overlooked. This pattern certainly exists, but it is not the only center about which the verse of the tragedy turns. The remarks of the other characters and of the choruses have long been thought of as goads to Samson's progress and as hindrances, too, but I am not completely convinced of this. Krouse has recently analyzed these tragic conditions in terms of an accepted theory of temptation which is illustrated in both *Paradise Lost* and *Paradise Regained*. For him Samson becomes intermediate in the chronology of Satanic enticements, and we as Christian readers are given a third and perhaps ultimate example of how we also may withstand the blandishments of evil.[9] The tragedy can be thought of in this way; in fact, it may be part of a tetralogy that includes *Comus*, but the temptations are somewhat different. So without rejecting any other explanations, I should like to shift the emphases a little because the artistic process that I notice in *Samson* centers on the regeneration of a desperate man and includes in its circular scope all of the theological dicta on the genesis and cure of despair.

When we study the documents in the Samson tradition, we are disturbed by one question that was constantly phrased and that makes the theological dissertations on this legend particularly unique. "Was Samson," the theologians ask, "a suicide and does his soul wander beyond the pales of mercy?" Though sometimes implicit, this question rests on Samson's last words which are recorded in the authoritative Hebrew text and expunged with vainly suppressed horror in the vernacular translations: "Let my soul," Samson prays as he braces himself between the pillars, "die with the Philistines." Either Samson did not believe in the after-life or he was praying, as a self-convicted suicide, for release from the pains of Hell. We can imagine the confusion of Christian men who could read the Hebrew; the passage must either be emended as a scribal error or sacredly misread. The controversy about Samson's suicide may be followed through the history of Christian hermeneutics, but there is no need to trace every step of the way in this essay since two contemporaries of Milton summarize the opposing cases. John Donne, by confuting the arguments of the orthodox,

[9] *Milton's Samson and the Christian Tradition* (Princeton, 1949), 124–32; see also Elizabeth Pope, *Paradise Regained: The Tradition and the Poem* (Baltimore, 1947), 51–107.

upholds Samson as the first of Biblical suicides and a justifier of self-destruction.[10] Franciscus Collius [11] gathers together the contrary testimony to show that Samson died a martyred avenger of Israel's Jehovah. Milton, we can be sure, knew this contention well, for he recognizes it poetically in the warning words that he places in the mouth of the aged and half-comprehending Manoa.

> Be penitent and for thy faults contrite,
> But act not in thy own affliction, Son;
> Repent the sin, but if the punishment
> Thou canst avoid, self-preservation bids;
> Or th' execution leave to high disposal,
> And let another hand, not thine, exact
> Thy penal forfeit from thyself (502–508).

But Manoa is wrong, for Milton's Samson, as Milton's Adam, is desperate and the desire to die is his, but death by suicide is never in his mind.

The eating despair of Samson is partially unveiled in his first speech where, unlike his prototype, he shows himself to be a man of " restless thoughts " that fill his mind with doubts. For what purpose, he asks himself, was I singled out, " separate to God," I who am " eyeless in Gaza at the mill with slaves? " This, to a reader of seventeenth century essays on Providence, is a familiar line of reasoning; it is the way the good man talks in his tribulations. Job asked questions of this sort, and Milton knew that it was the first move in the gambit of doubts about the wisdom and validity of Providence. For a moment Samson is on the edge of error, but he saves himself with a quick admonition. " But peace, I must not quarrel with the will/ Of highest dispensation " (60–61).

Yet there is a fluctuation throughout the early part of the tragedy in Samson's attitude towards himself, a fluctuation arising from the contention between his sense of sin and the fear that he has been abandoned by God. The seventeenth

[10] *Biathanatos* (London, 1648), 199–201.
[11] *De Animabus Paganorum* (Mediolani, 1622), 251–59.

century knew that the most righteous men were sometimes keenly aware of a separation from God, that even God himself could cry at the ninth hour, " Eli, eli, lama, sabachthani." But there is a difference between this feeling of desertion and the one that arises from a guilty heart; hence, Samson, as blind in eye as he was once in mind, has this more quickened conviction of abandonment.

With this the death-thought comes, for the darkness of his physical affliction symbolizes for Samson the darkness of the pit of death (100–104). His face becomes the mirror of his mind as the chorus sorrowfully describes him " As one past hope, abandon'd, and by himself given o'er." For these Hebrews of the year 1199 B. C. (I follow the chronology of Salianus) Samson appears, as mediaeval men were to see him, a broken giant from some titanic *de casibus virorum* (166–75). " Deject not then so overmuch thyself " (213). Samson hardly needs this advice; he blames himself for giving up his " fort of silence to a Woman," but he blames Israel more for hanging back when deliverance was at hand at Lehi. At this moment the inward undulation of Samson's spirit is upward, and this is good because Manoa's visit will once again bring him to the edge of the chasm of despair.

Manoa has much of the pessimism and some of the world pain of a man who has lived long and seen most of his hopes thin out; hence, he has become, as much as it is possible for a Jew, a pre-Stoa stoic who sees in withdrawal, in the quiet folding of hands, the decent and sensible conduct of life. From time to time his suffering finds voice: " And oh, what not in man/ Deceivable and vain! " (349–50). But love is strong in him for his strong son; it is, in fact, so strong that sometimes he doubts the justice of God (368–72). Wanting in a correct conception of God's wondrous ways, Manoa unwittingly substitutes himself for God, and seeks to persuade his son to accept the plans of a loving father instead of awaiting those of a loving God. If there is a temptation in this scene, it revolves about this substitute proposal. Had Samson, who has already fallen into sloth through lechery (Aquinas states that " *delectationes vereneae* " pave the way to sloth), accepted his father's plans, he would have plunged deeper in the slough of sloth. Yet Manoa, in his old man's fashion, goes beyond this. By implying that God has no further use for Samson, he presses his son against the sharp blade of despair. God, says Manoa who is truly more blind than Samson, will surely assert his might against Dagon;

> But for thee what shall be done?
> Thou must not in the meanwhile here forgot
> Lie in this miserable loathsome plight
> Neglected (478–81).

The ultimate victory of Jehovah is never doubted by either Samson or his father, but they are both totally unaware of the instrument of God's impending success. As a consequence of this ignorance, Manoa's love and devotion—emotions good in themselves—have the attributes of temptation, for the eventuation of these humanly good impulses is the thwarting of the divinely good.

During the whole of this first scene, Samson's self-accusations pile up. "Now I have sinned; now I am damned." Not the least among the items of his personal indictment is the feeling that his sick doubts have infected the nation whose champion he was.

> To *Israel*, diffidence of God, and doubt
> In feeble hearts, propense enough before
> To waver, or fall off and join with Idols (454–56).

Joined with this widening feeling of guilt is the lingering notion, for which Manoa is partly responsible, that God intends to punish him but not to employ him (487–501). When Samson puts this hard intimation into words, his father instinctively frames another temptation. By warning Samson against suicide, he puts the thought in his mind. But though Samson, at these words, begins to be hungry for " oft-invocated death "

and says of life " To what end should I seek it? " (522), he
prefers that death will find him worn out at the mill rather
than sitting in " sedentary numbness " at home. Neither suicide
nor sloth are in his mind.

Manoa is probably Milton's broadest irony. His well meant
attempts to alleviate the suffering of his son have invariably
an effect of contrary intent. The loving vision of a helpless
and hopeless idleness extending into a long old age that is his
only medicine for the convalescent Samson almost produced a
dangerous relapse.

> So much I feel my genial spirits droop,
> My hopes all flat, nature within me seems
> In all her functions weary of herself;
> My race of glory run, and race of shame,
> And I shall shortly be with them that rest (594–98) .

Once again Samson is beset by a " sense of Heav'n's desertion "
(632) and despair, black and ugly, fells him as no strong man
had ever done.

> Nor am I in the list of them that hope;
> Hopeless are all my evils, all remediless;
> This one prayer yet remains, might I be heard,
> No long petition, speedy death,
> The close of all my miseries, and the balm (647–51) .

So Samson reaches the bottom level of despair; he will never
again sink so low. The sickness is so regnant in him that its
contagion begets a similar disease in the chorus, the symptoms
of which are its complaint against the Jehovah who persecutes
his elect and its prayer that Samson may be spared. The complaint is artistically ironic because it exactly marks the point
in the tragedy where the regeneration of the protagonist begins.
The former emotional fluctuations of the hero will cease with
the last note of the choral song and Samson will move steadily
upward towards the elected event that will make him God's
martyred champion and one of the great prototypes of Christ.
The irony is not diminished with this scene for it permeates

the whole regenerative process, which depends not on the counsel of Manoa or the Hebraic chorus, Samson's friends and the children of Jehovah, but rather on the taunts of Dalila and Harapha, enemies of Israel and haters of Jehovah. For Milton, God had, indeed, a bitter sense of humor.

By refusing the lazy comforts offered by his father, Samson implicitly demonstrates that the love of God is to be preferred to paternal affection. The first enticement to sloth is forfended and with it the avenue to the damnable sin of despair is stopped. The same pattern of distraction from the foreordained triumph is poetically repeated in the scene with Dalila, save that in this episode the temptation is one of venereal love, that fostress of despair. This is an old weakness of Samson's; he had been tangled in it before.

But we cannot understand this episode in its full import unless we accept all that Dalila says as seriously spoken. Her final speech has always been allowed to color everything that she says, and this, I think, is not only a critical error in the commentaries, but a failure to read dramatically. When Dalila leaves the stage, she is a spurned beauty, a wife rejected. Her consolation, as she proclaims it, is the prospect of political renown. I see no reason, then, to assume that all of her speeches except the last are lies and that the whole purpose of her visit is to twit Samson. This would suggest that Dalila has a higher type of intelligence than that with which Milton ordinarily endows her sex. Shallow though she is, Dalila visits Samson out of contrition and remorse, her kind of contrition and remorse, but Samson himself knows that these emotions are but thinly part of her and that the real impulse is lechery.

> But Love constrain'd thee; call it furious rage
> To satisfy thy lust (836–37).

By rejecting her, Samson expiates, among other evils, his own history of lechery.

Every speech of Dalila's except the last is filled with verbal tones of contrition; and if we consider all of this spurious, we lose the intensity of the total contention. We must assume that while this charmer of charmers is speaking, Samson is aware of a strong physical attraction made more persuasive by redolent memories. The old passion is perhaps even more intense because now, for the first time, Dalila's natural gift for feminine cajolery and sweet words is enhanced by a feeling of guilt for her treachery and of sympathy for the betrayed. Granted that these emotions are all on the surface; nonetheless, they are as deeply felt as Dalila can feel. If we will be just a little tender with this " Hyaena," we can readily understand the pressures under which the fragile resistance of her slender intelligence collapsed. She wanted to know her husband's secret; she knew him to be a fickle lover; she feared for the seemingly reckless man who fought lions and armies single-handed; she was overwhelmed by the prestige of princes and archbishops, by Church and State. Eve betrayed her husband on the fair say-so of a beast of the fields and Eve was the nearest thing to feminine perfection that God ever created. Let us give Dalila a little chivalrous indulgence.

As *advocatus Dalilae* I may say still more. When Samson makes surly mock of her remorse and sarcastically shreds with his wise piety her self-exculpating brief, she patiently persists in her solicitations.

> Life yet hath many solaces, enjoy'd
> Where other senses want not their delights
> At home in leisure and domestic ease,
> Exempt from many a care and chance to which
> Eye-sight exposes daily men abroad.
> I to the Lords will intercede, not doubting
> Thir favourable ear, that I may fetch thee
> From forth this loathsome prison-house to abide
> With me, where my redoubl'd love and care
> With nursing diligence, to me glad office,
> May ever tend about thee to old age
> With all things grateful cheer'd, and so supplied,
> That what by me thou hast lost thou least shall miss

(915–27).

One can reasonably doubt whether a woman who came, as the critics say, to gloat over the misery of the husband whom she hated, a woman who did not believe in her own sincerity, would make such a selfless proposal to a broken and blinded man. We should also remember that her anger does not flare when Samson scornfully and even nastily rejects her offer. It is only when he spurns her last and, to her, most powerful enticement, physical contact (" Let me approach at least, and touch thy hand "), that she loses her rather remarkable self-control. To her complete confusion, she learns that she is physically repellent to Samson. For a wife or mistress this must be the ultimate insult. If we are to question any one of Dalila's announcements, it is the last one that she utters when she leaves the scene escorted by her wounded pride. The reward of a footnote in the history of the Phoenicians, which she says will now be hers, is sorry consolation, indeed, for the sort of woman who had been an international beauty.

The importance of this scene is manifest. Samson asserts himself against his first antagonist, and by this simple but energetic action the dejection, in which his interview with the comforting Manoa left him, vanishes. His uxorious weakness, the mother of much of his despair, goes with Dalila's exit. He has found the woman out, so he talks like a monastic brother. She is a Circe, who with her " enchanting cup, and warbling charms," has transformed him into a manless thing. She is a viper, too, a reptile that destroys her mate in the act of love. Samson discovers all of this as he struggles to free himself from the trap of Dalila's body. The chorus is not insensitive to the struggle.

> Yet beauty, though injurious, hath strange power,
> After offence returning, to regain
> Love once possest, nor can be easily
> Repuls't, without much inward passion felt
> And secret sting of amorous remorse (1003–1007) .

Samson feels these emotions, but he has withstood the solicitations of paternal affection and has less difficulty in rejecting

those of venereal love. He is walking towards purification and
the right understanding of the love of God, and in this scene,
he wins a test victory, the first of a series, against Dagon and
his vain adorers. I do not think that temptation is the basic
motif of this episode; it is intended as an adumbration of
Samson's ultimate triumph. Dalila is withstood, but we must
remember that both she and Harapha will finally be overwhelmed in the fall of Dagon's house.

During the subsequent scene with the giant Harapha,
Samson arises still higher in godly confidence and almost leaves
his original despondency behind. His contention with Dalila
enables him to suppress his erstwhile lechery; the conflict with
Harapha will enable him to subdue his apathy. Boughner sees
in this event a comic moment, a period of relief before the final
tragedy, and compares Harapha to the famous *milites gloriosi*
of literature.[12] In these comparisons he seeks a means of
enriching Parker's prior theory that Harapha was a blusterer
similar to those found in Greek and Latin tragedy.[13] I doubt
that Milton, who had complained in his preface about those
who " through the poet's error " intermixed " comic stuff with
tragic sadness and gravity," would make the same error himself.
I likewise doubt that Harapha is similar to Ralph Roister
Doister, his ancestors or his progeny. We should accept Milton's
prefatory remarks as sincere—Boughner does not—and, as a
consequence, we shall want Harapha to be as sincere as his
inventer.

If we will read without prejudgment, we will discover that
Harapha's first speech is that of a genuinely valorous man,
proud of his famous ancestry and of his long record in the
annals of war. We know his counterparts in the romances of
chivalry—knights who know their rivals by reputation but who
have never competed with them in the lists or on the fields of

[12] " Milton's Harapha and Renaissance Comedy," *ELH*, XI (1944),
297-306.
[13] *Milton's Debt to Greek Tragedy in Samson Agonistes* (Baltimore,
1937), 122.

honor. Harapha's visit to Samson is prompted by a champion's curiosity, and we should accept his first speeches as uttered honestly and generously. When he says he regrets that he cannot win honor from Samson in " mortal duel " because Samson is blind, he is not hedging but talking as a man conscious of the knightly code. If we insist that Harapha is a coward or a blusterer from the moment of his entrance, we fail to understand the essential purpose of the whole tragic situation. If, on the other hand, we admit his sincerity, the scene becomes infinitely important because we can watch the degeneration of Harapha's courage. Before our eyes a brave and knightly man will change into a coward and a blusterer. This amazing alteration in character, brought about by Samson's growing confidence in Jehovah and Harapha's intimation of the supernatural power apparent in Samson, tells us more than even the verse implies of God's impending triumph.

As Samson hurls challenge after challenge at Harapha, " his Giantship's " valour withers and he begins to think of all the excuses and dodges that had been used by generations of craven warriors to save themselves from an unlucky contest. The alteration in Harapha's nature is really a miracle which establishes its validity by taking place in our presence. The grand champion of Gath (and he did not get this title by bragging) turns into a snivelling bully-boy; Lancelot becomes Braggadocchio within the space of a hundred and fifty lines. Samson's confidence grows and Harapha's melts. To defend his own declining courage, Harapha uses some of the old arguments that had earlier cast Samson into despair. God has disowned you, says he,

> Thee he regards not, owns not, hath cut off
> Quite from his people, and delivered up
> Into thy Enemies' hand, . . .
> As good for nothing else (1157–59, 63) .

But Samson knows better now; the theme of divine abandonment has no effect. God, Samson intones, has afflicted me justly, but he has not deserted me:

> yet despair not of his final pardon
> Whose ear is ever open; and his eye
> Gracious to re-admit the suppliant;
> In confidence whereof I once again
> Defy thee to the trial of mortal fight,
> By combat to decide whose god is God,
> Thine or whom I with *Israel's* Sons adore (1171–77).

With this speech we know that Samson will not die an apathetic death. Life has returned to him; and though he does not yet know how it will all be brought about, he is God's champion once more. There is no temptation in this scene and no comedy; it is the most important scene of all, for it is the hinge of the tragedy. By the victory over Harapha, who symbolizes all that is valiant in Philistia, God, working through Samson, has put Dagon down. It is, in truth, the final event of the tragedy in miniature.

Now Samson's course is easy, for the way upward, the patient surrender to faith, once the obstacles in the hard lower levels are cleared, is as easy as the effortless descent to despair. Harapha is the dramatic link between the last breath of desperation,

> But come what will, my deadliest foe will prove
> My speediest friend, by death to rid me hence,
> The worst that he can give, to me the best (1262–64);

and the triumphant death, of which he is, perhaps, the bringer-on. " He will directly to the Lords, I fear,/ And with malicious counsels stir them up/ Some way or other yet further to afflict thee " (1250–52). Samson will still hesitate because he is a strict keeper of the Law, but his reasons for hesitation will vanish as soon as he, like the Christ of *Paradise Regained*, trusts again his inward impulses. " I begin to feel/ Some rousing motions in me which dispose/ To something extraordinary my thoughts " (1381–83). We know the nature of this " motion."

> And now by some strong motion I am led
> Into this Wilderness, to what intent
> I learn not yet; perhaps I need not know;
> For what concerns my knowledge God reveals
>
> (*PR*, I. 290–93) .

With these words God's athlete enters the ranks of the blessed.

Samson's God-given victory over Dagon and the flower of Philistia is, according to Milton's dramatic intent, not so great as Samson's conquest of doubt and despair. The final act stemming from this conquest destroys the universal doubt about the wisdom of God's Providence which had invaded Israel, the doubt for which Samson blamed himself in his earlier moments of dejection. The chorus exults in the clearing of this doubt and the final unfolding of God's plan, and in so doing exonerates the wrestler of God from the taint of suicide. " Among thy slain self-kill'd/ Not willingly, but tangl'd in the fold/ Of dire necessity " (1664–66) . Manoa, too, is purged of his dubious fears.

> And which is best and happiest yet, all this
> With God not parted from him, as was fear'd,
> But favouring and assisting to the end (1718–20) .

But there is more to the tragedy than the passionate purgation of the chorus, of Manoa, and of Samson. Aristotle may have laid down the rules and the poet Milton may have obeyed them, but behind them both was a greater critic and a greater poet who made the rules in eternity and supplied the tragic *fabula* for his own glory. Now that the happy catastrophe has occurred and the final chorus is sung, the candles are burning out in the long hall and the spectators are departing surer of the wisdom of the great artist whom Milton served.

> His servants he with new acquist
> Of true experience from this great event
> With peace and consolation hath dismist,
> And calm of mind, all passion spent.

V

DESCRIPTION AS COSMOS:

The Visual Image in "Paradise Lost"

TO SAY that a poet's imagery is the reflection of his satisfaction with his cosmology is to say nothing novel or intense, but in an age when cosmological points of view are either wanting or confused, it is, perhaps, important to say this repeatedly. The modern privation of belief and its consequent discomposure is made manifest in the non-monistic symbols, the private hieroglyphs of inner ignorance with which much of modern literature talks. The inner system is either the reflection of the outer one, or it is imposed on the outer one by an act of will. When both systems are incomplete or unassociated, expression becomes diaeretic. Modern man is his own world, for which he makes light by the generators of his inward darkness. With the possible exception of John Donne, this was hardly the manner of the seventeenth century, and Donne himself, we must remember, eventually called forth order from confusion though it never appears to have been a very comfortable kind of order. He was always unable to examine it from without and so it had the paradoxical quality of a homocentric metaphysics. It is for this reason that Donne was some years ago the hero of modern readers of poetry. Poets found him, in his early stage of uncertainty, imitable; critics discovered him to be congenially understandable. He was liked best at that point in his life when he was most confused.

Because Milton did not share this confusion, he has been abused for everything from his life to his Latinity. I shall not defend him at all points of attack, for it is not proper to my purpose to refute again the aspersions of Eliot, Leavis, Murry, and Cecil on his modes of poetical thought. Bush has done this far better than any other pro-Miltonist could.[1] Eliot has since recanted, but his recantation has much in common with some of the other famous recantations of history; it gives the impression of an embarrassed reluctance, a hesitant withdrawal to a point of further attack. In keeping with Eliot's new position, I wish once again to examine the nature of Milton's visual imagery and to do nothing more. In 1936 Eliot condemned it as insufficient; in 1947 he described it as " a positive virtue " when we enter the Garden where " a more detailed account of flora and fauna could only have assimilated Eden to the landscapes of the earth with which we are familiar." The imagistic pressure is light, " the light, which remembered by a man in his blindness, has a supernatural glory inexperienced by men of normal vision." On the other hand, " our sense of sight must be blurred, so that our *hearing* may become more acute," for Milton's " emphasis is on sound, not the vision, upon the word, not the idea." I cannot agree with the dogma of the last statement, but the total text of Eliot's second essay moves a little closer to what seems immediately true. If we would establish ourselves, as nearly as modern men can, in the Miltonic milieu, we should, perhaps, have a better understanding.

All visual imagery depends on words suggesting color, shape, and motion. The transference of the image from the bare words of the text to the imaginative faculty of the reader demands almost as much nervous energy as was expended by the poet in the original conception of the words. By selecting words of a more stimulating and precise quality and by setting them down in an extraordinary but not unnatural sequence, the poet performs the greater task, but the reader must exhaust an almost equal amount of mental tissue in completing what the poet has begun. Eliot vaguely denies this (though who

[1] *Paradise Lost in Our Time* (Ithaca, New York, 1945).

should know better than he) when he informs us that in Milton's poetry sound is superior to vision, words to ideas which are the coagulations of words. I should like to review this judgment in terms of a passage from *Paradise Lost*.

In the third book, we have our first view of Heaven, but we really know nothing about it until our reading is almost half done. The great apostrophe to light is followed by the unadorned speeches of God and Christ, unadorned because of a basic concept of the divine that I discussed in the introduction. Christ in his single courage volunteers to sacrifice himself for the preservation of his inferiors, blunting thereby the pseudo-sacrifice of the destroyer Satan. His decision is commended by the Father and for the first time we see the Kingdom of Heaven.

> No sooner had th'Almighty ceas't, but all
> The multitude of Angels with a shout
> Loud as from numbers without number, sweet
> As from blest voices, uttering joy, Heav'n rung
> With Jubilee, and loud Hosannas fill'd
> Th' eternal Regions: lowly reverent
> Towards either Throne they bow, and to the ground
> With solemn adoration down they cast
> Thir Crowns inwove with Amarant and Gold,
> Immortal Amarant, a Flow'r which once
> In Paradise, fast by the Tree of Life
> Began to bloom, but soon for man's offence
> To Heav'n remov'd where first it grew, there grows,
> And flow'rs aloft shading the Fount of Life,
> And where the river of Bliss through the midst of Heav'n
> Rolls o'er *Elysian* Flow'rs her Amber stream;
> With these that never fade the Spirits elect
> Bind thir resplendent locks inwreath'd with beams,
> Now in loose Garlands thick thrown off, the bright
> Pavement that like a Sea of Jasper shone
> Impurpl'd with Celestial Roses smil'd.
> Then Crown'd again thir gold'n Harps they took,
> Harps ever tun'd, that glittering by thir side

Like Quivers hung, and with Preamble sweet
Of charming symphony they introduce
Thir sacred Song, and waken raptures high;
No voice exempt, no voice but well could join
Melodious part, such concord is in Heav'n (344–72).

I have selected this description because, with few exceptions, it contains more word equivalents of color — gold, amber, jasper, and purple (probably red in the Miltonic eye) —than almost any other in the epic; yet it is almost without color, for those that are here summoned by word belong to almost the same grade in the spectrum. Gold, the metal of the sun, the symbol of " Holy Light " suffuses the whole scene with shadow variants of amber, jasper yellow or brown, and the red of ancient purple. But the similarity of the color scale or color-lessness itself has really no part in the possessive richness of the description, for we are overpowered, as we are expected to be, by an unlimited cascade of light. This is both the essential light of God and the infused light by which his creatures shine. Song is here too, we are told, but we do not hear it in the mind until the passage consequent to the description is made intelligible. Vision and vision alone invades us.

We are aware at once that we are not looking at a single canvas but at a triptych painted with lucid symbols that provide the vision with a spiritual significance. In the first panel, as our eyes move down the printed page, we see angels in many postures of adoration bowing before the dual throne of God, " casting down their golden crowns upon the glassy sea " and their flowery garlands as well. In the third panel the serviceable angels are crowned and stand among immortal roses as they sing with one voice to the harp. The center panel is Paradise symbolically described. The amarant grows by the Tree of Life and is watered by the Fountain of Life. In the foreground the River of Bliss " rolls o'er Elysian Flow'rs her Amber stream." What is absolutely expressed in this center of symbol is expounded modally in the pictures to right and left. We should be detained by the central panel first.

The visual image suggested by the word *flower* dominates either generically or specifically the whole metrical concourse; the triple panels have this symbol as one of their unifying elements. In the static central panel the generic word is made specific in the history of the amarant, which is not a real flower at all but an ideality inexpressible in terms of earthly flora. The author of Genesis when he described the temptation of Eve used a Hebrew word for *fruit* that means a sensuous combination of all the beguilements of taste, color, and fragrance. The celestial flower, long lost from the gardens of this world, is invented in the same way from the Greek ἀμάραντος, a word used in Scripture for the Christian concept of spotlessness. As a consequence, this flower, beyond the things of earth, has neither color nor form: it is an emblem of immaculateness enhancing the visual interpretation of the accompanying panels and lifting them above a mundane commentary.

It is this concept of stainlessness that brings out the power of the immortality symbols that crowd the remainder of the middle panel: the Tree of Life, the Fountain of Life, and, in a way, the combination of the two in the life-giving river that flows eternally over its flowery beds, reminding us of the certainty of resurrection. Here is life without end, the eventual awakening to life, the sense of a felicitous infinity, but all of these prospects are supported by the doctrine of immaculateness revealed in the purity of essential light. The center never changes. It is as quiet as God. By implication, however, it overflows into the two angelic pictures.

We do not see an angel, for they are " numbers without number," and this opening description moves triumphantly towards " such concord is in Heaven." The infinite number of angels have so put their hearts together (con + cordia) that they are as one. Immortal spotlessness becomes, in the final sublimation, celestial unity. This transmutation is annotated here, in the language of reverent adoration, by the idea of obedient worship. Stasis vanishes, and though we never see a single angel, we have an unbelievable sense of angelic movement. We are conscious of the ceremonious change and interchange of courtly gesture; we watch the bright diadems and the floral chaplets as they fall before the throne of God. Then our eyes move and we see the vast polyphonic choir of harpers celebrating God and his works. Motion and light, not color and shape, make the portrait of Paradise. The angels move and our eyes move, but the double movement has a single symbolism. From the devout obedience of infinite number we and they pass into the realm of an immaculate eternity so that in the end the many is received into the one, " such concord is in Heav'n."

This is a high sort of visual description, and Milton was able to do this because he was not in revolt against tradition. His cosmology enabled him to accept the tradition and widen it. Eliot's allusiveness makes his poetry intelligible only to men as well-bred as he; Milton may talk about " fit audience but few," but his definition of the universe was generally understood. By elaborating one aspect of this definition, I shall apologize for my previous explication and make a further point about the Miltonic devising of visual imagery. Some Miltonists have not been unaware of the importance that light and its qualities played in this poetry, but the emphasis has been placed totally on the poet's want of vision. This, I think, is not wholly true. If we know something about Renaissance theories of light and light symbolism, we shall be assured that the avoidance of it was for Milton poetically impossible. This is not the time for a large dissertation on the matter; [2] hence, I shall confine myself to what Ficino said at the end of the fifteenth century—for here Platonism is mingled with mediaeval doctrine —and to what Kircher, the Lord Acton of the age, wrote during Milton's life.

Light, which the seventeenth century thought of as first form and motion—Grimaldi likens it to the fluidity of music [3]—

[2] K. B. Collier, *Cosmogonies of Our Fathers* (New York, 1934), 338–50 *et passim*.

[3] *Physico-Mathesis de Lumine* (Bononiae, 1665), 396–420.

appeared to Milton's contemporaries as a graduated divine impulsion, "descendens a Patre luminum," who was himself symbolized by essential light, " th' Eternal Coeternal Beam." Ficino expands the theories of the Middle Ages, perceiving many analogies between light itself and the Father of Lights, for the very form of the word, φώτων, as St. James uses it, suggests a palpable gradation. Ficino thinks that it is almost as impossible for mortals to comprehend the true nature of light as it is for them to know the symbolic Divine Light. It exists through itself and incorporeally in itself, but as it descends from the fountain of light, it assumes materiality, it becomes clouded and shadowy. Hence we see light through a blurring window as a scale of opacities. The same is true of the *lumen divina*, but here we may rise by a ladder of light to an almost complete comprehension of its real source.[4] What Ficino says is repeated with the advantage of a better science by Kircher in 1646.

Essential light cannot be seen by men towards whom it descends, Kircher writes, because it is hindered and refracted by the many media through which it passes. The light that the angels see as a blinding whiteness, Shelley's " white radiance of eternity," is broken by the intervening media into colors—redness for men, blackness for beasts. " No light," as Milton says of Hell, was there " but rather darkness visible." Light which in God is supercelestial, *lux*, and *lux perpetua* is for man, dwelling within his murky dome, shadow, clouds, and twilight.[5] Man lives, then, in an evening world and what he sees as colors are simply the broken shafts of the eternal ray. The nature of Milton's visual imagery is expounded by these opinions. The colors and shapes with which poets of the Renaissance adorn their descriptions are a confession of imperfection, the direct result of the privation of the essential light, which suffers the fate of forms and loses its perfection as it unites with matter.

4 *Liber de Lumine* in *Opera* (Basel, 1561), I, 976–84.
5 *Ars Magna Lucis et Umbrae* (Romae, 1646), 917–24.

We cannot, therefore, expect the precision of imagery that we find in Shakespeare, whose cosmology, as his themes, was certainly more homocentric, in the poet to whom this world was already dim and shaded before blindness made it dark. We must remember, too, that in *Paradise Lost* we are being led through a world that is still bathed in essential light, so we shall have to think in metaphors of white splendor, in similes of motion, not in those of color or sharp edges, the figures of a post-lapsarian cosmos.

Though Milton is no less sparing in his use of color than Donne, it is on light and its derivative manifestations that his major imagery rests. Of this we are continually reminded. The great encomium of light with which the third book of *Paradise Lost* opens makes the three-fold distinction between essential light, material light, and the Divine Light by which inwardly the poet sees. The primeval light with which its material manifestation, the sun, is nurtured, is described in the seventh book. Throughout the whole poem blessedness is associated with the complete comprehension of the increate light, the essence of immaculateness. Its " sacred influence " pours over the walls of Heaven (II. 1034–40), and the battlements of Paradise are approached by a drawbridge of light (III. 510–18). The creatures who people the City of God are " Progeny of Light " (V. 600) or " Sons of Light " (XI. 80). This is Biblical phrasing but it is in keeping with the nature of God, *Pater luminum*, and of Christ, *Lux mundi*.

> Fountain of Light, thyself invisible
> Amidst the glorious brightness where thou sit'st
> Thron'd inaccessible, but when thou shad'st
> The full blaze of thy beams, and through a cloud
> Drawn round about thee like a radiant Shrine,
> Dark with excessive bright thy skirts appear,
> Yet dazzle Heav'n, that brightest Seraphim
> Approach not, but with both wings veil thir eyes.
> Thee next they sang of all Creation first,
> Begotten Son, Divine Similitude,

> In whose conspicuous count'nance, without cloud
> Made visible, th'Almighty Father shines,
> Whom else no Creature can behold; on thee
> Impresst the effulgence of his Glory abides,
> Transfus'd on thee his ample Spirit rests (III. 375–89).

Absence from God is symbolized throughout the epic by a privation of light, and it is often the darkness rather than the pains of Hell that oppresses its remorseful inhabitants so bitterly. The mind of Satan is troubled with trying recollections of a brighter world: " the happy Realms of Light " (I. 85), the " dreary Plain . . . void of light " (I. 180–82), " this mournful gloom/ For that celestial light " (I. 244–45), the long, hard way that " leads up to light " (II. 433). The lecturers in Pandæ-monium cannot stay off the subject any more than their leader; Belial (134–37, 220), Mammon (262–73), and Beelzebub (397–402) remember light wistfully as a good that has slipped from them. We could have anticipated their unhappy remarks, for in their foolish attempts to imitate Heaven in Hell, they have tried to dispel the blackness of their sub-human life with fueled lamps that simulate those that burn before the throne of God.

> Pendant by subtle Magic many a row
> Of Starry Lamps and blazing Cressets fed
> With *Naptha* and *Asphaltus* yielded light
> As from a sky (I. 727–30).

In spite of this artificial blaze, the citizens of this gas-light metropolis yearn for the perpetual white clarity that once they knew; Satan may curse the sun, but he curses it in envious recollection of the time when " cloth'd with transcendent brightness " he outshone " myriads though bright."

Satan's defiance to the sun with its implied defiance of God emphasizes this envious yearning because Satan has visited the world of the sun on his journey to Eden. He approached it through a rhythmic maze of dancing lights which " Turn swift their various motions, or are turn'd/ By his Magnetic beam "

(III. 582–83). When he checked his flight, the movement of the shining bodies was transformed into a bright effluence as Milton distilled the speculations of the astronomers to a poetic essence. The visual imagery of this description is as plain as the sun itself. The eyes of the demon sweep over the florid ground thick with bright minerals. What he sees reminds us, as readers of the Old Testament, of the breast-plate of Aaron with its mysterious center stone, unknown to the commentators but thought by some to be the long sought *lapis Lydius*. The similar recollection of this by Milton begets the alchemistic metaphor with its innumerable solar associations. Then, as Satan, in keeping with the chemical trope, watched the rising exhalations in the major laboratory of life, he saw, as a Christian would expect, the angel of St. John. This is most important, for the allusion looks forward to Satan's final defeat and destruction, of which, at the moment, he is unaware. To us it is an affective figure, for the brightness of the angel, in keeping with the theories of the gradation of light, outshines the splendor of the great material creature by which the lesser creation sees.

Since Heaven is filled with " Light unsufferable " and Hell is a " dark opprobrious Den," earth, though far brighter then than now, is an empire of half-lights, as misty a world as the one Adam saw from the hill of the " Visions of God." We see the sublime garden of the world through the darkened eyes of cormorant Satan, who views it from his ironic perch on the Tree of Life. In this description of eighty lines, we see little that is particularized by name—palms, roses, grape vines, and myrtle—much that is generalized and allusive. The subsequent account of the nuptial bower, though shorter by far, is as detailed as Marvell's garden:

> it was a place
> Chos'n by the sovran Planter, when he fram'd
> All things to man's delightful use; the roof
> Of thickest covert was inwoven shade
> Laurel and Myrtle, and what higher grew

Of firm and fragrant leaf; on either side
Acanthus, and each odorous bushy shrub
Fenc'd up the verdant wall; each beauteous flow'r,
Iris all hues, Roses, and Jessamin
Rear'd high thir flourisht heads between, and wrought
Mosaic; underfoot the Violet,
Crocus, and Hyacinth with rich inlay
Broider'd the ground, more colour'd than with stone
Of costliest Emblem (IV. 690–703).

It is evident that when we view the bower through the still sinless eyes of Adam and Eve, we see each plant in particular, but the shades that the sinful demon sees are wanting. Satan sees color—" vegetable Gold," " gay enameld colours mixt," " Golden Rinde," " Purple grapes "—but this squinting vision fails to make specific distinctions because white radiance is no longer his.

Throughout *Paradise Lost* we live in a world of light until the Fall; then for the first time we see night as we know it. Yet the pure light that shines through most of the first nine books is varied as a descriptive agent by the metaphoric qualifications of motion. We are sometimes puzzled to know how this is done. Perhaps the characters move; perhaps we and the poet, who moves us, move. At any rate, by light and motion Milton creates an effective visual imagery that is somewhat different from what we, as belated Elizabethans or ordinary moderns, have known. His method differs definitely from that of his literary predecessors, Donne, Shakespeare, and Spenser. To consolidate his images Donne uses real objects that continue to function in the real world and startle his readers by their reality. The reason for his success as an unconventional poetic improviser rests in the fact that his readers were accustomed to the counters of analogy that Shakespeare and Spenser pay down. Though Donne sometimes uses these counters, he got them at a different treasury. This minted language of analogy enchanted the Elizabethans, as it does us after we memorize it, because, unlike Donne's ordinary tongue, it is a poetic language rather than an actual one. In the world of reality the Elizabethan might have different emotional reactions to the king and to the sun, but in the world of poetry he saw them as metaphoric equivalents. Neither of these imagistic methods is strong in Milton, whose visual imagery is likely to be based on a spatial sense rather than on local habitation. A further requirement is that it be partially supported by the reader's learned, but not necessarily logical, imagination, meditating richly on the affective suggestions of the poet.

It is motion in full brightness that enlarges the extended descriptions of the epic, and Adam in his morning hymn gives us a text which may be applied in this aesthetic consideration just as truly as it may be urged with Godlike irony against the most mobile member of the cast: " Rising or falling still advance his praise " (V. 191). This is the essential plight of Satan (though Moloch has argued that up and down do not matter), who is the most carefully watched and closely described of all the epic characters. From direct metaphoric statement we know that Satan is gigantic when he wishes, that he has a crime-washed countenance, that he has unbridled passions and a confused mind. This might be enough, but we know still more about him because we have seen him moving across the face of the newly created cosmos. His constant restlessness, as a matter of fact, is a prime exposer of his godly pretensions, for he is as opposite to God in his mobility as he is in all other ways.

The first book of *Paradise Lost* measures the satanic proportions by a series of similes that have not recently been admired by Milton's disparagers. These similes were part of the traditional epic baggage and as such were suited to the seventeenth century's sense of antiquity; nevertheless, the great bulk of the fallen archangel is more vigorously and imaginatively described when he " rears from off the Pool/ His mighty Stature." The Himalayas of flame surge back and roll in vast billows. It is an explosion in a titanic volcano; the launching of a mighty rocket. The images associated are those of an earthquake or a convulsion of Aetna, but we hardly need them. When we see Satan thus in motion, we are told more about the horrible size of the red monster than all comparisons of shield and spear and island length can possibly yield. A similar explosion enforces this realization of immeasurable size when, in book four, the demon toad bursts at the touch of Ithuriel's spear like a depot of powder and fills the whole scene with his shocking limbs. The unparalleled force of expansion besets us, for in the sigh of a moment he has burgeoned from a reptile that one can hold in the hand to a threatener larger than the Colossus at Rhodes. But Satan is also described by his travels.

While Milton moves us from Hell to Earth to Heaven to Earth to Hell, Satan accompanies us in a steady course of rise and fall with which his mind keeps unequal balance. We invariably see him at distances, for as a moth on a glass window he surges into chaos to fall ten thousand fathoms and ascend again on a cloud of nitrous fire. After his seemingly successful diplomatic mission to the old anarch, he springs " like a Pyramid of fire/ Into the wild expanse " (II. 1013–14), and we watch as he hurtles towards earth " in many an Aery wheel " (III. 741). He is never still; restless, a great bat he speeds round the earth, and, finally, reducing his size to that of a mere mote, pounces, stalks, and writhes. It is this diminution that convinces us, for now we know that we have not been observing Satan against a handful of sky as we might observe an eagle, but against the total area of the universe. To have seen him so plainly in this immensity, even though he seems no larger than an insect, is a terrible testimony to his inexpressible proportions. The simile suits the end, for we see him descend to Hell, gliding between the Centaur and the Scorpion " while the Sun in *Aries* rose " (X. 329). We know him at last, a baleful comet presaging doom to men, but frustrated by the sign of Easter and the risen Son of God.

It is not only Satan who is made visible by motion; whole scenes are made flesh by this forceful use of verb. Perhaps the most successful is the description of the imperial review in the

first book, a poetic panorama from the pencil of a baroque
painter.[6] The picture assembles itself slowly as the long procession of demons wearing their evil aspects like crowns and
carrying their savage histories like flags advance with weary
and half-conscious steps towards the middle ground. The
motion is hesitant and horizontal, but suddenly there is a
quickening of movement and the vertical takes pre-eminence.
It all happens quickly. Azazel unfurls the king's standard.

> Th' Imperial Ensign, which full high advanc't
> Shone like a Meteor streaming to the Wind
> With Gems and Golden lustre rich imblaz'd,
> Seraphic arms and Trophies: all the while
> Sonorous metal blowing Martial sounds:
> At which the universal Host upsent
> A shout that tore Hells Concave, and beyond
> Frighted the Reign of *Chaos* and old Night (I. 536–43) .

Our eyes leave the colorless laggards, for they are dazzled by a
massive blast of light that streams across the heavens, whereas
at the same time our ears are conquered by the identifiable
tones of "sonorous metal blowing Martial sounds." While
we are transfixed by this alteration of motion and light, the
tempo assumes a rapid beat.

Either the picture begins to move towards us or we, who
have been at the far end of the gallery, move quickly towards
the picture as the single banner that first distracted our attention is joined by ten thousand others and then by a forest of
spears. The vertical that was empty is suddenly used up by
continual motion and by frequent imaginative shifts of light.
Now we see more clearly the " thronging helms " and " serried
shields in thick array." By some magic we have moved more
closely without knowing it and we are, for the first time,
examining the vast armies with a particular eye. While we
move, the host of Hell moves towards us " in perfect *Phalanx*

---

[6] This text was suggested by A. Stein, " Milton and Metaphysical Art,"
ELH, XVI, 120–25.

to the *Dorian* mood." The unaccorded trumpets' clangor and the great humanlike shout give way to the order of music. The warriors who have marched irregularly in single file, then massed with only the motion of their flaming banners and waving spears to hold our eyes, now assume the order of perfect march, silent, determined. Suddenly we are no longer in motion, for we are part of the picture, not spectators at all, and the well disciplined divisions that have been marching towards us have halted. We are no longer idlers in a baroque art museum; we are he at whose command the mighty host waits.

It requires more than the prescribed relaxed mind to become part of Milton's visual imagery because it must be understood in large and not in detached words and phrases. This is the way that Milton saw the world, and he sharpened his human sight on his conception of his universe. Given a similar understanding and a mind tolerant enough to supply the unexpanded terms of his description, it is not difficult to see as well as hear.

VI

REALIZATION AS CLIMAX:

"Paradise Regained"

IT IS difficult not to read *Paradise Regained* as an immediate poetical continuation of *Paradise Lost*, but if we indulge in such a reading, if we constantly return to *Paradise Lost* for annotations, we confuse our judgment of the short epic and distort, if we do not destroy, the central issues of the second poem. *Paradise Regained* is not Books XIII to XVI of *Paradise Lost*; it is not a true sequel of Book XII, nor is it a commentary on the high acts in Heaven of Book III and the sorrowful episode on earth of Book XI. The nature of the " exalted man " should in no way be compared with that of the " Begotten Son, Divine Similitude." The temper of the weary but clever Satan is by no means that of the newly fallen archangel and novice tempter of Eve. What Milton constructs in *Paradise Regained* is a totally new dramatic epic describing a contest between an antagonist and a protagonist whom we have never before seen.

The Satan of *Paradise Regained* is not only millenniums older than the Satan of *Paradise Lost*, but he is, unlike his predecessor, almost completely lacking in physical dimensions. He is a creature of the middle air, whereas the Satan of *Paradise Lost* dwelt in the republic of fire, a salamander then, an evil Ariel now. As befits his long experience, the new antagonist takes at first the form of an old man, but custom conquers and he quickly assumes his wonted shape. He is the Mephistopheles of Marlowe and Goethe; the suave man of the world well-

known in every court of Europe. Even with this, we know little
more about him. We never see his haunted face, his desperate
eyes, his tired mouth twisted by two thousand years of cynicism.
He has laid aside his familiar weapons, his plumes, his rays,
his sinister badges of office. He has become, in this new state,
pure mind—the hard, treacherous mind of evil.

The mind of this different Satan seems at first to be strangely
uncertain, but this uncertainty is really a pretense. In his
vicious masquerade, Satan begins by claiming to be ignorant
of his opposite although he has clear intelligences augmenting
the ancient memories of the earlier sentence of the judgment
in Eden. Is this unusual man " His first-begot," he asks, or is
he mere man, " for man he seems? " The question, if it is a
question at all, is answered at first encounter: " Knowing who
I am, as I know who thou art " (I. 356). Satan does not pause
for explanation but at once admits with devilish sophistication
his prior intuitions. " 'Tis true, I am that Spirit unfortunate."
But for diplomatic reasons, perhaps, he still maintains the
illusory doubt. At the beginning of the second conclave, he so
persists in this false ignorance that he makes an unlikely comparison between the dangerous new opponent and the old
Adam, and so succeeds, by hiding his own perfect realization,
in misleading the single-minded Belial.

> Though *Adam* by his Wife's allurements fell,
> However to this Man inferior far
> If he be Man by Mother's side (II. 134–36).

The real doubt that lurks in the mind of the " old Serpent "
is about his own failing powers as a corrupter and not about
the identity of his opposite.

The reiterated and insincere uncertainty of Satan is, first,
a method of heartening his colleagues, but he quickly discovers
its use as an implement of seduction. Throughout the epic
he pretends to doubt who Christ is in order to establish a mood
of self-distrust in the mind of the " exalted man." He begins
almost at once, for the first temptation, though it has strong

physical implications, is soundly based on the unsettling ques·
tion of election: " What proof have you that you are favored
of God? " The approach, which becomes formularized, is filled
with speculative innuendoes.

> For that to me thou seem'st *the man* whom late
> Our new baptizing Prophet at the Ford
> Of *Jordan* honour'd so, and call'd thee Son
> Of God (I. 327–30).

We shall hear the same quizzical tone break through the screen
of Satan's practiced subtilties at many moments in the remaining three books. " Declar'd the Son of God " (I. 385) ; " But
much more wonder that the Son of God/ In this wild solitude
so long should bide/ Of all things destitute " (II. 303–305) ;
" Be not so sore offended, Son of God,/ Though Sons of God
both Angels are and Men " (IV. 196–97) ; " For Son of God
to me is yet in doubt " (IV. 501). This series of sly doubts,
cunningly sarcastic at times, twists to the inevitable false
syllogism,

> The Son of God, which bears no single sense;
> The Son of God I also am, or was,
> And if I was, I am; relation stands;
> All men are Sons of God; yet thee I thought
> In some respects far higher so declar'd (IV. 517–21) ;

and explodes in the futile desperate attempt: " Cast thyself
down; safely if Son of God " (IV. 555). Yet Satan in his heart
of hearts is never in doubt.

It is fear, cold fear, rather than uncertainty that is the major
quality of the evil mind of *Paradise Regained.* In one instance
of supreme blandishment, evil can skillfully pretend to a desire
for reconciliation with good:

> though to that gentle brow
> Willingly I could fly, and hope thy reign,
> From that placid aspect and meek regard,
> Rather than aggravate my evil state,

Would stand between me and thy Father's ire,
(Whose ire I dread more than the fire of Hell)
A shelter and a kind of shading cool
Interposition, as a summer's cloud (III. 215–22) .

Now this tender of submission is from the human point of view
very touching, for we know that demons in torment pray hopelessly, but Satan's contrition is patently false. He has already
announced that where hope is gone, " is left no fear " (III. 206)
and expressed a desire to " be at the worst." These are, then,
contrasting emotions that do not complement each other. To
wish to be at the worst consorts illy with the hopes of temptation; to be without hope, when hope is the whole content of
the action, is equally incompatible. It is fear of the worst that
governs the disturbing processes of the mind of evil, for fear,
as sin, is both the spouse and child of evil.

In his first report to the aery synod, the cold damp of fright
covers all the words that flow from Satan's mouth. " His birth
to our just fear gave no small cause " (I. 66) , but, he adds,
thirty years of miraculous growth in wisdom and virtue have
multiplied these fears until " Ye see our danger on the utmost
edge/ Of hazard, which admits no long debate " (I. 94–95) .
The first test that follows this convocation augments the satanic
fear to such a degree that the demon, defeated in the prelimi-
nary exchange of grips, returns ostensibly to seek further advice
but really to prepare his powers for ruin. His confidence,
fattened by generations of easy success, has withered and all
Hell is put on the alert (II. 143–46) . The temptation of the
banquet, the last of the sensual efforts, shows in its elaborateness
the full extent of this terror. Satan no longer can trust in a
crude apple or in the compelling pangs of forty days of hunger;
he must turn out his pockets in such a vast effort that temptation is destroyed by its own surplusage. The fear that brings
this flaw in the technique of temptation is increased by the
words of the Son of God, for we must not fail to notice that
Christ tempts Satan, if Satan can be tempted, both to anger

and fright. There is an explicit violence in " My time I told
thee (and that time for thee/ Were better farthest off), is not
yet come " (III. 396–97) ; there is a prophetic threat in " What
if I withal/ Expel a Devil who first made him such? " (IV.
128–29). After this, Satan, who for political reasons has been
an humble and patient flatterer, replies " with fear abasht "
(IV. 195) and smashed in the center of his pride, boasts of his
crumbling empire in the shuddering manner of a king on the
eve of revolution. " Who then thou art, whose coming is fore-
told/ To me so fatal, me it most concerns " (IV. 204–205).
With these words he admits that his doom is read.

Such is the early evidence of Satan's fear, but we see it at
its greatest pitch when it turns to a panic that drives him to
violence. At the first conclave Satan had assured his followers
that he would not use force against the " exalted man." " Not
force, but well couch't fraud, well woven snares " (I. 97). Yet
as the well-planned enticements of wealth, of power, and of
knowledge fail as readily as the limited and absurd temptations
of appetite, Satan is driven to strike out with all his harsher
powers. He becomes an infernal poet and writes in Nature a
violent version of " Il Penseroso ":

Darkness now rose,
As day-light sunk, and brought in louring night,
Her shadowy off-spring, unsubstantial both,
Privation mere of light and absent day.
Our Saviour meek and with untroubl'd mind
After his aery jaunt, though hurried sore,
Hungry and cold betook him to his rest,
Wherever, under some concourse of shades
Whose branching arms thick intertwin'd might shield
From dews and damps of night his shelter'd head,
But shelter'd slept in vain, for at his head
The Tempter watch'd, and soon with ugly dreams
Disturb'd his sleep; and either Tropic now
'Gan thunder, and both ends of Heav'n; the Clouds
From many a horrid rift abortive pour'd
Fierce rain with lightning mixt, water with fire

In ruin reconcil'd: nor slept the winds
Within thir stony caves, but rush'd abroad
From the four hinges of the world, and fell
On the vext Wilderness, whose tallest Pines,
Though rooted deep as high, and sturdiest Oaks
Bow'd thir Stiff necks, loaden with stormy blasts,
Or torn up sheer: ill wast thou shrouded then,
O patient Son of God, yet only stood'st
Unshaken; nor stay'd the terror there.
Infernal Ghosts, and Hellish Furies, round
Environ'd thee, some howl'd, some yell'd, some shriek'd,
Some bent at thee thir fiery darts, while thou
Sat'st unappall'd in calm and sinless peace (IV. 397–425).

Undaunted by the fact that God opposes a quiet "L'Allegro" to his lines of horror, Satan reiterates his doubts about whether the " exalted man " has the favor of God (IV. 470–73, 514–21). When these doubts again effect nothing, he admits what clearly he has long known: " Thou art to be my fatal enemy " (IV. 525). This supreme admission of what Christ had long before read in the mind of evil produces the supreme violence, for when Satan sets Christ " on the highest Pinnacle," it is poorly concealed murder and nothing else that he has in mind. Until this last attempt, all the temptations of *Paradise Regained* have been based on besotting the mind of good because when he was perfectly in control of his faculties, Satan knew that the calm chance of success resided in this. But fear and panic have thrown him down, and in these two final acts of violence, he tosses away the elaborate plan of his great campaign and at last reveals himself as a cornered and desperate animal.

If there is uncertainty in the characters of *Paradise Regained*, it is to be found not in Satan but in Christ, in the proto-disciples, and in the Virgin. It is not the uncertainty of ignorance, such as that which has been attributed to Satan, but rather a sacred unknowingness, an eager expectancy made staunch by the surety of promise. We meet it first in Andrew and Simon, who begin " to doubt, and doubted many days,/ And as the

days increas'd, increas'd thir doubt" (II. 11–12). Yet their
doubts, it must be remarked, are not those of the spiritually
miserable since the text informs us that they are seekers and
that the object of search is better to hear the divine truth
faintly murmured. To this end they are resolved to let "his
Providence" assume the weight of their fears:

> he will not fail
> Nor will withdraw him now, nor will recall,
> Mock us with his blest sight, then snatch him hence,
> Soon we shall see our hope, our joy return (II. 54–57).

The Virgin, too, has a large share in this holy expectancy, and
though she may for a moment yield to sorrows "and fears as
eminent' (II. 70), yet it has been a succession of glorious
experiences from which she has gained sublime patience to
await the "strange events" (II. 104).

The uncertainty of the Virgin and of the future disciples
arises really from an ignorance of the true mission of the
"exalted man." Andrew and Simon, who are learned in the
lore of the rabbins in spite of their humble origins, assume
that Christ is the Messiah who will restore the material throne
of Israel and free the Chosen People from the yoke of stranger
kings. The Virgin hardly has this illusion, but she cannot
fathom the "great purpose." She has the elder Simon's
prophecy in her heart and it lies there like a sharp sword,
portending affliction and sorrow. Satan alone, I think, knows
the nature of the mission from the beginning, knows its true
import though he is ignorant of the details; but Satan has a
remembrance of history that the human members of the epic
lack. For this reason, it is the uncertainty of Christ that lies
behind the single action of the poem and that fits the parts
of the *fabula* together.

In poetically evoking the figure of the tempted Christ,
Milton was faced with an almost insuperable artistic obligation.
Christ could not be shown as totally conscious of his godliness
because this would not only violate the strictures of theology

but spoil the intense nature of the epic struggle. On the other hand, Christ cannot be presented as simply human, even as the best of all possible men, for the mysteries of the Incarnation and the understood doctrine of hypostasis declared otherwise. The figure of Christ surpasses all the traditions of artistic imitation, and it became Milton's almost impossible poetic task to illustrate the unillustratable. There is no doubt in my mind that he failed—no one could write the part—yet he succeeds better than we, on occasion, are inclined to admit. It is exactly at this point of our critical considerations of *Paradise Regained* that we do well to forget the existence of *Paradise Lost*, for if we remember the Christ of book three, we are unlikely to see the temptation as anything more than a formalized set piece. We must, consequently, think of the " exalted man " as forgetful of his divinity, of his victory in Heaven, of his sacrificial offer, or of its foreordained fulfillment. Christ, at the beginning, is only the " exalted man," triumphant in virtue and wisdom, and filled, as his precursor Samson, with a sense of election and high favor.

In order to turn our imaginations in a new direction, Milton, early in the epic of *Paradise Regained*, takes us to Heaven and writes for us a scene that is quite detached from those of *Paradise Lost*. The speech of God to Gabriel, the annunciator, contains no ancient memories of earlier events in Heaven. The predictions of God are given to the angel as totally new. The *man* born of the Virgin, God says, has now grown and I shall expose him to the wiles of Hell.

> He now shall know I can produce a man
> Of female Seed, far abler to resist
> All his solicitations, and at length
> All his vast force, and drive him back to Hell,
> Winning by Conquest what the first man lost
> By fallacy surpris'd (I. 150–55) .

This man, God adds, will now " lay down the rudiments/ Of his great warfare " (I. 157–58) by which he will overcome evil

so that all may know " From what consummate virtue I have
chose/ This perfect Man, by merit call'd my Son " (I. 165–66).
The purpose of this scene is that we may start afresh, helped
by a set of conditions different from those of *Paradise Lost*. We
are told that a duel is about to begin that will be worth watch-
ing; but since we must watch it as men, it is a man whom we
shall see.

The fluctuation in this man's knowledge of himself and of
his mission is what makes *Paradise Regained* more taut in
action than Johnson perceived. In his divine nature Christ
knows his identity and foresees his course, but in his human
nature the " exalted man " is often uncertain of both. As we
read the epic, we watch him as he crosses and recrosses the
boundary between the two persons, for it is out of this wandering to and fro, out of the humanly uncertain and the divinely
sure that Milton gives validity to the test and extracts from it
a highly dramatic conclusion. It is also Milton's way of ex-
pressing the union of the two natures in Christ, and we can
hardly expect him to succeed where almost two thousand years
of theology had failed; nonetheless, he comes closer to explaining this concept poetically than any other poet—for that
fact, almost any divine—who had attempted it before.

In order that we may understand the humanity of Christ,
Milton has used two devices that are dramatic rather than
epic. He has given us the inner conversations of Christ with
himself in which humanity prevails and he has given us the
untrustworthy doubts of Satan about the divine favor and
origin of the Son of God. We know the latter method already
and the former will be quickly comprehensible if we overhear
the meditations of Christ as he is led into the wilderness and
analyze his resumé of his continued speculations about his
nature and his life purpose. As Christ reads his autobiography,
we trace with him the alterations in his understanding. We
learn that he once thought of himself as a man-at-arms eager
to free Israel from the Roman yoke and suppress universal
tyranny, " Till truth were free." Then he turned to wisdom

and to the persuasions of the public teacher; " By winning words to conquer willing hearts,/ And make persuasion do the work of fear " (I. 222–23) . He is at once assured and perplexed by the strange wonders that attended his birth and illuminated his growth to manhood, but he is at this time as uncertain of their interpretation as Satan, the master astrologer, will eventually be of what he reads " in the Starry Rubric set." In some way the sins of man will be visited on him, but he has forgotten the merciful event in Heaven. He knows only that he stands on the threshold of an extreme expectancy, the time

> Now full, that I no more should live obscure,
> But openly begin, as best becomes
> The Authority which I deriv'd from Heaven.
> And now by some strong motion I am led
> Into this Wilderness, to what intent
> I learn not yet; perhaps I need not know;
> For what concerns my knowledge God reveals (I. 287–93) .

It is amazing how strongly the undefined expectations of the human Christ flare into divine certainty whenever he is confronted by the subhuman enticements of the mind of evil. This seems almost to be the pattern. When Christ is alone, he is human; when he is confronted by Satan, he assumes divinity or, at least, is raised above humanity. On these occasions Christ not only knows himself, but remembers the long history of his opponent both in Heaven and in earth. The sheer ecstacy of spirit that kindles the " exalted man " smites the demon with fearful humility.

> But thou art plac't above me, thou art Lord;
> From thee I can and must submiss endure
> Check or reproof, and glad to scape so quit (I. 475–77) .

What is described in book one is repeated in book two, for once again, after the first victory, we find Christ alone, uncertain, unknowing, but not untrusting. " Where will this end? " he asks himself, and although he does not admit it, his

dreams suggest a hope of divine intervention. Yet when Satan
appears with his resplendent and aromatic feast, Godliness is
at once made manifest.

> I can at will, doubt not, as soon as thou,
> Command a Table in this Wilderness (II. 383–84).

Satan, as we know, is well aware of this crossing and recross-
ing of the barriers of humanity and plays many variations on
it. He is not ignorant either of Christ's inner speculations on
the nature of his mission. He knows that the " exalted man "
once held before himself the violent prospect of liberating
Israel and the world by force of arms or by political arrangement. This awareness of Christ's secret thoughts comes out in
the shrewdly integrated temptations of wealth and power by
means of which he attempts to draw Christ back to his human
side and to use for evil ends his human uncertainty.

> Thou art unknown, unfriended, low of birth,
> A Carpenter thy Father known, thyself
> Bred up in poverty and straits at home;
> Lost in a Desert here and hunger-bit (II. 413–16).

He continually attempts to increase the mortal sense of personal
unimportance and insufficiency, reminding Christ, as Milton
had once reminded himself, of the blossoming worldly careers
of younger men, of Philip, Scipio, Pompey, and Caesar. By
these historical comparisons he attempts to reduce Christ to
wavering humanness. Finally, when all these efforts come to
naught, when his grand spectacle of the teeming world has
faded to nothingness before Christ's intenser consciousness of
his mighty mission, Satan turns to the ultimate temptation of
wisdom in which the mind is tempted by itself. But Christ,
the Light of the World, knows how pale the Light of Nature
is before the great illumination of the Inner Light.

As Satan's fears increase and as he exhausts the quiver of
the temptations, Christ's sense of his own divinity increases
and the human side of his nature becomes more obscure. Now

at last he knows that his kingdom has no place in the records of time: "And of my Kingdom there shall be no end" (IV. 151); now at last he is sure that all that is is his: "As offer them to me the Son of God,/ To me my own" (IV. 190–91). He has, in the end, a full understanding of his extra-human human nature, for he scorns the demon's absurd claim of worship.

> And dar'st thou to the Son of God propound
> To worship thee accurst, now more accurst
> For this attempt, bolder than that on *Eve*
> And more blasphemous? (IV. 178–81).

All of this leads up to the Biblical finale, for only one more rebuff is needed: "Thou shalt not tempt the Lord thy God." The full concept of God-in-man is rounded out with this. While hovering between his human and divine natures, Christ has withstood a series of human temptations far greater than those offered any other man, but to tempt God is the peak of futility. The temptation recoils, as it had in the history of the Jews, on the tempter himself.

Christ's calm recognition of his divine nature and his ultimate mission, "*Eden* rais'd in the waste Wilderness" (I. 7), is reexpressed in the great climax with which the epic ends. History restates itself and Satan falls before the Son of God, repeating his defeat at the beginning of the world. The angelic hosts appear (the fiery globe that surrounds God in Heaven) to hymn the victory of Christ and to predict his remaining task. He can now go forth, certain of his nature, remembering his assumed duties, and fully assured of his celestial powers. He is no longer Christ, hovering between the human and the divine, but God in man, "heir of both worlds," a spirit in, but above, flesh, who has tasted "Fruits fetcht from the tree of life,/ And from the fount of life Ambrosial drink" and has heard the "Heavenly Anthems of his victory."

VII

THE DESCENT TO LIGHT:

Basic Metaphor in "Paradise Lost"

THOUGH THE English Protestants of the seventeenth century were, to their ultimate spiritual distress, so devoted to the literal interpretation of the Bible that they considered it the primary and superior reading, their affection for the letter and the historical sense did not prevent them from searching the text for types and allegories. This practice, of course, bore the taint of popery and hindered the full powers of the *fides divina*; yet it often yielded excellent results and enabled one to skirt the marsh of a troublesome passage. Though not addicted to the allegorical method, Milton was no stranger to it. He might scorn Amaryllis and Neaera, but he could spend an occasional moment of leisure with what Luther called " these whores of allegory." The latter books of *Paradise Lost* and the tragedy of *Samson* proved that he was quite a talented typologist, who could find foreshadowings of the great Advocate of Grace in the biographical records of the advocates of the Law. More than this, Milton, unlike many of his contemporaries who were inclined to be universal in their analogical researches, made fine discriminations between types because he believed in what we might now call " typological evolution."

An example of Milton's interpretative discretion is his refusal to accept—although in this he was contrary to theological

Reprinted from " Milton Studies in Honor of Harris Francis Fletcher," *Journal of English and Germanic Philology*, LX (1961) , 614–30, with permission of the University of Illinois Press. Originally titled " Milton and the Descent to Light."

opinion—the patriarch Aaron as a full type of Christ. He contended that this first priest simply adumbrated the priestly offices of Jesus.[1] When he came to this conclusion, Milton was flatly correcting the assertions of the Anglican prelates; but on another similar occasion he was mentally flexible enough to correct himself.[2] Since he also believed in a dynamic typology that changed as the sacred history was unrolled, he was quick to admit that symbols valid before the Law[3] were afterwards worthless.[4] He could also insist on the gradual revelation of types and symbols because he believed that the thunder and trumpets' "clang" on Mt. Sinai proclaimed, among other things, a new form of typology and established Moses, who was, in a guarded sense, "the Divine Mediator" and "the type of the Law,"[5] as a master typologist. This evaluation had more than human worth because it was Jehovah who instructed Moses so that he could teach this mode of interpretation to men.

> Ordaine them Lawes; part such as appertaine
> To civil Justice, part religious Rites
> Of sacrifice, informing them by types
> And shadowes, of that destind Seed to bruise
> The Serpent, by what meanes he shall achieve
> Mankinds deliverance (*PL*, XII. 230–35) .

These words are placed in the mouth of the Archangel Michael, who at this moment is manipulating the magic lantern of holy shadows and who is also an experienced exegete skilled in all four senses. Shortly after speaking this gloss, he announces that the main purpose of the Old Testament is to prepare the sons of Adam for a "better Cov'nant, disciplin'd / From shadowie Types to Truth, from Flesh to Spirit" (XII. 302–303) . The mighty angel thus suggests that man can ascend (as humbled Adam has ascended from the Vale of Despond to the Mount of

---

[1] *Church Government, Works* (New York, 1931–38) , III, 202–205; hereafter I shall cite only volume and page.

[2] *Hirelings*, VI, 55, 58; *Christian Doctrine*, XIV, 311.

[3] *Christian Doctrine*, XVI, 191.

[4] *Ibid.*, XVI, 197.

[5] *Ibid.*, XVI, 111.

the Visions of God) from the darkness of sin and ignorance into the light of truth, from the shadow of type and symbol into the white blaze of the eternal literal.

It must be confessed that typology, even at its finest, is little more than hindsight prophecy; it points surely to the Advent, but it is best understood when the Word is made Flesh. Allegory—a game that even Jehovah plays[6]—is, in Milton's somewhat reluctant opinion, a possible form of revealed knowledge. This knowledge may be useful in some instances and not in others. When, for example, Moses urges the Israelites not to plow with an ox and an ass, Milton, who has been searching Deuteronomy for divorce evidence, perceives that the Hebrew lawgiver has the Miltons in mind,[7] an interpretation that speaks better for a sense of mystery than for a sense of humor. In his poetry Milton uses allegory with somewhat better artistry than a modern reader might imagine. An illustration of this skill appears when he shows Satan, orbiting in space and viewing the margin of Heaven and the angelic ladder of which " Each stair mysteriously was meant " (III. 516) . By reminding us that Jacob's ladder had allegorical force, Milton prepares us for Raphael's subsequent description of the *scala perfectionis*, " the common gloss of theologians." There is likewise poetic irony resident in the fact that Satan, who is totally without hope, is permitted to see what will be interpreted as Adam's way of assuming angelic nature.

In general Milton probably defined allegory as a downward descent of knowledge, a revealing of suprarational information that enabled the humble learner to ascend. Raphael's well-known comment on his account of the celestial battles (V. 570–76; VI. 893–96) and Milton's open admission that he can only accept the six days of Creation allegorically (VII. 176–79) make the Miltonic conception of allegory plain. For the poet, allegory is the only means of communication between a superior mind aware of grand principles, such as the enduring war between Good and Evil, and a lesser mind incapable of higher mathe-

[6] *Ibid.*, XV, 145.
[7] *Doctrine and Discipline*, III, 419; *Colasterion*, IV, 265.

matics. It is essentially a form of revelation, or, as Vaughan would put it, " a candle tin'd at the Sun."

To burnish this observation, I should like to point to events within the confines of the epic that could be called an allegory about allegory. This sacred fiction begins to be written in Book II when Satan, leaving Hell for Eden, retains, except for his momentary ventures into several forms of symbolic wildlife, the literalness of satanship, never putting on the ruddy complexion, the horns, hoof, and tail by which he was recognized in the allegorical world. The celestial messengers, however, are real creatures and stay feathered and decorous so that Adam, unlike his sons, does not " entertain angels unawares." It is otherwise with Satan's strange relative, Death. At first he " seems " to be crowned and to shake his ghastly dart; actually, he is a vast black shadow, formless, not " Distinguishable in member, joynt, or limb, / Or substance " (II. 668–69). He is by no means the symbolic person who writes the dreary colophon to all human stories or who is stonily portrayed in ecclesiastical monuments. Once he has crossed his bridge into our world, he is better known. Although he is " not mounted yet / On his pale horse," we are familiar with his " vaste unhide-bound Corps " and we understand his hearty hunger for whatever " the Sithe " of his companion Time " mowes down " (X. 588–606). The bridge between the two worlds is a convention of infernal histories; but in *Paradise Lost*, it could also be called the Bridge of Allegory.

There is no doubt that at times Milton read the Scriptures for meanings other than the literal one, but he also was aware, thanks to a long tradition, that the pagans had a glimmer of Christian truth. Their lamp was scantily fueled and the wick smoked, but with proper adjustments it could be made to give off a " pale religious light." It took almost four centuries to light this lamp in the Church; the pagan philosophers and their idolatrous legends had first to be suppressed. Then, taking over the methods of the same heathen brethren, the Christian scholars began searching the mythology for physical, moral, and spiritual notions that had been bequeathed to men by the sons of Noah. The moral commentaries of Bishops Fulgentius and Eustathius on pagan literature encouraged others to unshell these truths, and in Renaissance England Chapman, Bacon, Reynolds, Sandys, Ross, and Boys searched the pagans for what had been better revealed in the Bible or was narrated in the Books of Creation. All of them were infected to some degree with the current confidence in a universal philosophical system, a disease nourished by earlier mystagogues such as Ficino, Pico della Mirandola, and Agostino Steucho, and best known to us in the fine clinical case of Theophilus Gale. Given the virulence of the epidemic, we are, consequently, not surprised when the daemon from " the threshold of Jove's Court " touches on it.

> Ile tell ye, 'tis not vain or fabulous
> (Though so esteem'd by shallow ignorance)
> What the sage Poets taught by th' heavenly Muse,
> Storied of old in high immortal verse
> Of dire *Chimaeras* and enchanted Isles,
> And rifted Rocks whose entrance leads to Hell,
> For such there be, but unbelief is blind (*Comus*, 512–18).

After reading this speech in *Comus*, we understand why the mythological remembrances in *Paradise Lost* are sometimes more than ornamental, why their submerged moral or spiritual meanings enable them to consort with and support the braver Christian myths. The multicolored phoenix, first underwritten by Clement of Rome as a Christ symbol, adorns Milton's own adventual allegory: the descent of Raphael through the air, " a *Phoenix*, gaz'd by all " (V. 272). Eden, expressed in vegetable grandeur, is quickly seared with evil foreboding when Milton likens it to the meadows of Enna, those sinister fields " where *Proserpin* gath'ring flow'rs / Herself a fairer Flow'r by gloomy *Dis* / Was gather'd " (IV. 269–71). When Milton compares Adam and Eve to Deucalion and Pyrrha (XI. 8–14), even we do not need a whole series of pious mythologizers to make the point; and foolish Pandora hardly needs the testimony of a Father as old as Tertullian [8] to inform us that she is the pagan half-memory of silly Eve (IV. 712–19). Milton is quite conven-

---

[8] *Liber de Corona, Patrologia Latina*, II, 85.

tional in permitting pagan legend to lend its soft biceps to Christian power. His method of searching for metaphoric support in heathen culture also enables him to stand aside from the other characters of the epic and act as a commentator on the pre-Christian world from the vantage point of a postclassical man. Among the various pagan figures with whom Milton plants his poetry, two rise above the rest; they are the poet-theologian Orpheus and the demigod Hercules. Both are attractive to him because of their Christian meaning.

From the flats of the first *Prolusion* through the latter ranges of *Paradise Lost*, Milton accents the legend of Orpheus in a way that suggests self-identification. The Greek hero was praised in antiquity and by men of later ages for softening the human heart and turning it through his higher magic to the useful and the good.[9] Christian as these achievements were, Orpheus, as Milton knew, enlarged them by singing of Chaos and Old Night and by teaching Musaeus the reality of the one God. St. Augustine, a Father beloved by Milton when he agreed with him, complained that Orpheus' theology was very poor stuff;[10] but other primitive theologians from Athenagoras onward hailed the Greek as unique among the unelect in explaining divine matters as a Christian would.[11] There is, as I have said, little doubt that Milton thought of the murdered poet as one of his own grave predecessors, and this view was probably enhanced by that of the Christian mythologists who described Orpheus as a pagan type of Christ.[12]

Clement of Alexandria is the first to bring both harrowers of

[9] J. Wirl, *Orpheus in der englischen Literatur* (Vienna and Leipzig, 1913). Milton's orphic imagery has been studied by Caroline Mayerson, "The Orpheus Image in Lycidas," *PMLA*, LXIV (1949), 189–207. The Columbia *Index* may be consulted for Milton's references to Orpheus.

[10] *Contra Faustum, PL*, XLII, 282; *De Civitate*, XVIII. 14.

[11] *Legatio pro Christianis, Patrologia Graeca*, VI, 928.

[12] Fulgentius, *Philosophi Mythologiarum libri tres* (Basel, 1536), 77–79; Berchorius, *Metamorphosis Ovidiana Moraliter* (s.l., 1509), fol. lxxiii; Boccaccio, *Della Genealogia degli Dei*, tr. Betussi (Venice, 1585), 87; dell'Anguillara and Horologgi, *Le Metamorphosi* (Venice, 1584), 357, 387; Comes, *Mythologiae* (Padua, 1616), 401–402, 548; Ross, *Mystagogus Poeticus* (London, 1648), 334–37.

Hell together, although his comments are actually an angry rejection of pagan complaints about Christian imitativeness. He brands the Christian doctrines of Orpheus as spurious and mocks the alleged majesty of his songs; then he turns with a " not so my singer " (ἀλλ' οὐ τοιόσδε ὁ ὁδὸς ὁ ἐμός) to praise the new Orpheus, who tamed the lions of wrath, the swine of gluttony, the wolves of rapine.[13] Religious Eusebius makes a similar comparison in a more kindly fashion:

> The Saviour of men through the instrument of the human body which he united to his divinity shows himself all saving and blessing, as Greek Orpheus who by the skillful playing of his lyre tamed and subdued wild animals. The Greeks, I say, sang of his miracles and believed that the inspired accents of the divine poet not only affected animals but also trees who left their places at his singing to follow him. So is the voice of our Redeemer, a voice filled with divine wisdom which cures all evil received in the hearts of men.[14]

The history of Orpheus as a pagan type of Christ can be traced for many centuries;[15] by Milton's time it was such a part of the symbolic fabric of Christianity that one had only to think of " lyre " to say " cross." It is, for example, Orpheus who comes into John Donne's mind when he writes in " Goodfriday," " Could I behold those hands which span the Poles, / And tune all spheares at once, peirc'd with those holes? " This is the occasional image of Christ on the lyre, but the open comparison is conventionally stated for us by Giles Fletcher:

---

[13] *Cohortatio ad Gentes, PG*, VIII, 56–57.

[14] *Panegyric to Constantine, PG*, XX, 1409.

[15] Lampridius informs us in his life of Alexander Severus (a work cited by Milton in *Of Reformation*) that this Emperor erected shrines to Abraham, Christ, and Orpheus: see *Historiae Augustæ Scriptores* (Frankfurt, 1588), II, 214. Antonio Bosio has a chapter on why Christians compared Orpheus and Christ in *Roma Sotterano* (Rome, 1630). For an account of the Orpheus-Christ metaphor in Spanish literature see Pablo Cabanas, *El Mito de Orfeo en la literatura Española* (Madrid, 1948), 153–76.

Who doth not see drown'd in Deucalion's name
(When earth his men, and sea had lost his shore)
Old Noah; and in Nisus lock, the fame
Of Sampson yet alive; and long before
In Phaethon's, mine owne fall I deplore:
But he that conquer'd hell, to fetch againe
His virgin widowe, by a serpent slaine,
Another Orpheus was the dreaming poets feigne.[16]

Thus Christians hallowed Orpheus for his half-success as a saviour of men and for his frustrated attempt to lead a soul out of Hell's darkness.

Tatian, in his *Oration Against the Greeks*, had argued that Orpheus and Hercules were the same person;[17] Milton would hardly say this, though he found in the demigod foreshadowings of both Samson and Christ. His admission of the Christian Hercules to his pantheon begins with the " Nativity Ode," where we are shown the infant Jesus " in his swaddling bands " ready to control the snaky Typhon and the rest of " the damned crew." It is Hercules, too, who is praised in *The Tenure of Kings* for his suppression of tyrants,[18] a superb Miltonic exploit; and he is recalled in the twenty-third sonnet for his rescue of Alcestis from the dark floor of Hell. He was, of course, attractive to Christians for other reasons. Begotten by Jove of a mortal woman, he early chose the right path, eschewing " the broad way and the green "; and, according to the almost Christian Seneca, " Jove's great son " devoted his whole life, in the best Stoic manner, to the conquest of his passions and the suppres-

---

[16] *The Poetical Works*, ed. F. Boas (Cambridge, Eng., 1908), I, 59–60. One of the earliest English comparisons is found in Gavin Douglas: see *Poetical Works*, ed. Small (Edinburgh, 1874), II, 18. Wither objects to these comparisons in *A Preparation to the Psalter*, 1619 (Spenser Society, 1884), 77–78.

[17] *PG*, VI, 885.

[18] *Op. cit.*, V, 19; for other references to Hercules see the Columbia *Index*. The Samson-Hercules-Christ identification is explored by Krouse, *Milton's Samson and the Christian Tradition* (Princeton, 1949), 44–45.

sion of vice.[19] His major exploits were against the forces of darkness. We first hear of him in the *Iliad* (V. 397) as he strikes Hades with his "swift arrow" to leave him in anguish among the dead. No wonder that he thrice descended into Hell with somewhat better fortunes than those of Orpheus.

When Milton read the Orphic poems, he read the one that praises Hercules as a human saviour, but the comparison between Christ and Hercules, like the comparison between Christ and Orpheus, had been made before Milton's birth. "Ipse Christus verus fuit Hercules, qui per vitam aerumnosam omnia monstra superavit et edomuit."[20] The analogy was firmly established across the Channel, where Hercules Gallus was a stern rival of Francus, by d'Aubigne's *L'Hercule Chrestien*,[21] a moral prose on the labors Christianly read. This book inspired the *Hercule Chrestien* [22] of Ronsard, who advises his reader to swim a little below his surface:

> Mais ou est l'oeil, tant soit-il aveugle,
> Ou est l'esprit, tant soit-il desreigle,
> S'il veut un peu mes paroles comprendre,
> Que par raison je ne luy face entendre,
> Que la plus-part des choses qu'on escrit
> De Hercule, est deve a un seul Jesuschrist.

Chaplain Ross, a good Scot, can put it bluntly: "Our blessed Saviour is the true Hercules."[23]

---

[19] *Dial.*, II. 2. 2; see also Apuleius, *Florida*, 14, and Servius on *Aeneid*, VI. 119–23. The moral mythologers who read Christ into Orpheus also found the same connections between Christ and Hercules: see Fulgentius, 32, 39–42; Boccaccio, 210–14; Gyraldus, *Hercules*, in *Opera* (Leyden, 1696), I, 571–98; Alciati, *Emblemata* (Leyden, 1593), 50–54, 505–508; Valeriano, *Hieroglyphica* (Basel, 1556), fols, 23^v, 109^v, 247^v, 386; Comes, 272–74.

[20] G. Budé, *De Asse et partibus* (Paris, 1532), p. lxix.

[21] *Oeuvres*, ed. Reaume and de Caussade (Paris, 1877), II, 226–31. Annibal Caro writes the Duchess of Castro: "Sotto il misterio d'Ercole si dinota Cristo, il quale estrinse il vizio, come Ercole uccise Cacco" (*Lettere Familiari* [Padua, 1763], I, 253).

[22] *Oeuvres*, ed. Vaganay (Paris, 1924), VI, 137–45.

[23] *Op. cit.*, 169.

There is little question that these two pagan Christ-types were congenial to Milton not only for their Christian grace notes but for their reflection of Miltonic ideals. Both heroes were received in the " sweet Societies / That sing, and singing in their glory move," because, as Boethius made clear,[24] they early chose the proper ascent to Heaven. Their accomplishments and their exploits were the sort that Milton himself might read in his own book of hope. But there is more to it than this. Hercules and Orpheus were types—not so good as Moses or Enoch, of course—of the strong Son of God and the Singer of the New Song. The event in their story that tied the hard knot of analogy was their descent into the darkness, their triumphs or half-triumphs in Hell, and their return into the light and, eventually, to the holy summits. In this process of descent and ascent, of entering the dark to find the light, the two halves of the coin of allegory were united.

II

The visual imagery of *Paradise Lost* depends to some extent on verbs of rising and falling, of descent and ascent, and on contrasts between light and darkness. These modes of expression coil about the demands of the central theme as the serpent coils about the forbidden tree so that we may be urged to abandon the horizontal movement of human history for the vertical motion of the spiritual life, the dark nothingness of ignorance and evil for the light of ultimate truth and reality. The descent of Milton into the darkness of Hell before he rises to the great " Globe of circular light " is a sound Christian rescript. " Descend," says St. Augustine, " that you may ascend." " Descende ut ascendas, humiliare ut exalteris."[25] Christ's double descent—first into the flesh and then into the dark Saturday of Hell—furnished those who humbled themselves with a map of Christian progress. One goes down in humility into the dark so that

[24] *Consolations*, III, met. 12; IV, met. 7.
[25] *Sermo* CCXCVII, *PL*, XXXIX, 2313–14; *Confessiones*, IV. 12; *De Civitate*, VII. 33; *Enarratio in Psalmos PL*, XXXVII, 1596–1600, 1606.

one may ascend in triumph to the light. Satan and his squires know this course well enough to pervert it.

When the black tyrant, who has been " Hurl'd headlong " down, addresses his companions, he pretends, contrary to fact, that the descent was voluntary and a preparation for ascension. " From this descent / Celestial Virtues rising, will appear / More glorious and more dread than from no fall " (II. 14–16) . Satan's prideful qualification is enough to make the word *rising* ironic; but his falsehood is not only believed but seconded by the deluded Moloch, who describes with desperate wit the millions that " longing wait / The Signal to ascend " and boastfully asserts " That in our proper motion we ascend / Up to our native seat: descent and fall / To us is adverse " (II. 55–77) . Moloch's knowledge is no better than his grammar, for he, like his fellows, has gone about it the wrong way. He has already ascended in pride; been guilty of a " sursum cor contra Dominum,"[26] and so he has " frozen and fallen like a flake of snow."[27] The literature of the Church knows all these phrases for the fate of the prideful aspirant; it tells us that those who descend in humility arise to those heights. " Unde Satan elatus cecidit, fidelis homo sublevatus ascendat."[28] The humble ascend to the light; the proud enter the depths, the "caligo tenebrarum densissima." [29] For those in hope of seeing the light that Satan truly detests, the road is easily followed, because both roads, as Bernard of Clairvaux puts it, are the same:

> The same steps lead up to the throne and down; the same road leads to the city and from it; one door is the entrance of the house and the exit; Jacob saw the angels ascending and descending on the same ladder. What does all this mean? Simply that if you desire to return to truth, you do not have to seek a new way which you do not know, but the known way by

[26] *Sermo* XXV, *PL*, XXXVIII, 168.
[27] *In Job, PL*, XXXIV, 875.
[28] Cassiodorus, *Exposition in Psalter, PL*, LXX, 1036.
[29] Anselm, *Liber de Similitudinibus, PL*, CLIX, 664–65.

which you descended. Retracing your steps, you may ascend in humility by the same path which you descended in pride.[30]

Augustine's descent in humility is paralleled by Bernard's descent in pride, because both are dark ways that lead upward to light. Had Milton's Adam been humble in obedience, he would have ascended, as Raphael, who had read the Church Fathers,[31] made plain (V. 490–505). But Adam sacrificed his prospects of angelic perfection for the immediate rewards of romantic love; even then, however, his subsequent humility guarantees his ascension. The demons also talk of ascending, but " self-tempted," they are secure in their fall. The bitter pride and the prideful unrepentance that governs them is embossed by Satan in his soul-revealing soliloquy:

> O foul descent! that I who erst contended
> With Gods to sit the highest, am now constrain'd
> Into a Beast, and mixt with bestial slime,
> This essence to incarnate and imbrute,
> That to the hight of Deitie aspir'd:
> But what will not Ambition and Revenge
> Descend to? who aspires must down as low
> As high he soar'd . . . (IX. 163–70) .

Satan, in other words, knows the rules. In time his legions will rise far enough to occupy the middle air, but they will not advance into the " precincts of light." Depth and dark are really their " native seat." Their master is very honest about this, admitting, as he returns from the grand seduction, that he finds descent " through darkness " an easy road (X. 393–98) .

It is darkness, as well as descent, even though it is "darkness visible " that plagues the newcomers to Hades. They sit in the gloom, as Gregory the Great tells us, " inwardly dark amidst the

---

[30] *De Gradibus Humilitatis*, ed. Burch (Cambridge, Mass., 1940) , 176.

[31] For patristic comments on the perfectibility of an unfallen Adam, see Hugo of St. Victor, *De Vanitate Mundi, PL*, CLXXVI, 723; St. Thomas, *Summa*, I. 102. 4; Pico della Mirandola, *De Hominis Dignitate*, ed. Garin (Florence, 1942) , 104, 106; J. Donne, *Sermons*, ed. Potter and Simpson (Berkeley, Calif., 1953–60) , II, 123, VII, 108.

everlasting darkness of damnation."[32] Behind them are "the happy Realms of Light" (I. 85), which they have exchanged for a dreary plain, "void of light" (I. 180). Once they were famed as God's "Bright-harness'd Angels"; now they spend their time plotting how to "affront" God's holy light "with thir darkness" (I. 389–91), confounding "Heav'n's purest Light" "with blackest Insurrection" (II. 136–37). In alternate moments they console themselves with foolish or violent plans for an escape to light (II. 220, 376–78), but Satan, who has read the sixth book of the *Aeneid*, reminds them that "Long is the way / And hard, that out of Hell leads up to Light" (II. 432–33). In Satan's church—and theology informs us that he has one—this might be called the diabolique of darkness; the counter-Church opposes to this opaqueness the sublime metaphysic of light.

We need not scratch through the Bible or the smaller gravel of the theologians to find the moral interpretation of the blackness of Hell, of the mind of evil, or what Milton's Jehovah calls the "dark designs." The Christian conscience is fully aware of the dark symbols. Ignorance, sin and sinner, damnation, Hell and its provost are festooned with black against a midnight ground, and the speculations of Beatus Jung are seldom required to expound the Christian tradition. Opposed to this night of negation is what might be called the *tenebrae in bono* which is consonant with the descent in humility and is explained by the divine darkness that even Mammon knows.

> This deep world
> Of darkness do we dread? How oft amidst
> Thick clouds and dark doth Heav'n's all-ruling Sire
> Choose to reside, his Glory unobscur'd,
> And with the Majesty of darkness round
> Covers his Throne; from whence deep thunders roar
> Must'ring thir rage, and Heav'n resembles Hell?
> As he our Darkness, cannot we his Light
> Imitate when we please? (II. 262–70).

[32] *In Ezechielem, PL*, LXXVI, 1290.

If these were not English devils, we would put this down to conscious humor; but the absence of jest is proclaimed when Pandaemonium is lighted with sputtering gas lamps that badly imitate Heaven's essential light. The dark with which God mantles himself is as different from Hell-dark as Hell-fire is from Heaven's blazing cressets. Moses, who ascended Mt. Sinai to enter the dark folds of God's light, could lecture the swart Mammon in hermeneutics.

Though Orpheus and Hercules enter the dark and arise to the light, the basic Christian idea of the dark god in the divine night is a totally different concept. For the ancients, light was the essence of existence and the sun shone in their temples, bathing the clear gods in bright gold. Death was the greatest of horrors, not because it deprived one of limb and motion but rather because it extinguished the mortal world of light. Dying Antigone weeps because never again will she see the holy light (879–80), and her lamentation is heard again and again in Greek tragedy.[33] Light was life, and it was also wisdom. For Plato φῶς is the means by which men who live in the realm of shadow almost place their hands on the unknown and unknowable.[34] The Roman stoics soothed themselves with the same consolation of light; hence Seneca can remind the suffering Helvia that " The gleams of night " enable one to commune with celestial beings and keep one's mind " always directed toward the sight of kindred things above."[35] The Christians, too, saw Jehovah as a bright God, the Father of Lights, and in his human manifestation, the *Lux Mundi*,[36] but they also knew him as a god in darkness,[37] assuming his cloak of clouds.[38] The figure of

[33] See also Sophocles, *Aias*, 854–65, *Oedipus Col.*, 1549–51, and Euripides, *Iph. Aul.*, 1281–82, 1506–1509.

[34] *Republic*, VI. 508–509, VII. 518; *Phaedo*, 99; see J. Stenzel, " Der Begriff der Erleuchtung bei Platon," *Die Antike*, II (1926), 235–37.

[35] *Ad Helviam*, VIII. 5–6; see also Plutarch, *De Genio Soc.*, 590 B.

[36] Psalms 36:9, 104:2; Wisdom, 7:21–25; I Timothy 6:16; I John 1:5.

[37] Exodus 20:21, II Chronicles 6:1, II Samuel 22:12, Psalms 18:11–12, 97:2, Job 22:14.

[38] Ezekiel 1:4, Revelation 1:7.

a darkened god visible only in the soul's night demanded an explanatory inscription on the entablature.

The Christian doctrine of the light in darkness begins when Philo Judaeus, the stepfather of exegesis, interpreted Exodus 20:21. The broad cloud on Mt. Sinai, he writes, is the allegory of Moses' attempt to understand the invisible and incorporeal nature of Jehovah;[39] it is also, in a more general sense, the symbolic exposition of the process by which the contemplative mind tries to comprehend the immaterial.[40] More than a century later, Roman Plotinus compared man's perception of common experience to wandering through the statues of the gods that crowd the outskirts of a temple.[41] The luminous soul has, truly enough, descended into darkness [42] when it has entered the flesh, but it still provides an inner light.[43] Once it has reached its limit this light is also changed into an obscurity;[44] but this limit does not blind the inner sight by which one may ascend to the light in the shadows (ἐλλαμψις ἡ εἰς τὸ σκότος) , the spiritual habitation which is the goal of the wise.[45] Philo, accounting for the experience of Moses, and Plotinus, elaborating on the light metaphysic of Plato, offered to western man an esoteric explanation of divine light: it hides itself in the dark and one must enter the cloud to find it.

Milton, who had only the rudimentary chronology of his age to guide him, would probably think of Plato as a contemporary of Moses. He would certainly accept the Pseudo-Dionysius, the great exponent of this philosophy, as the disciple of St. Paul and the coeval of Philo. He would, consequently, assign all these similar doctrines to the first Christian era. The facts, as we now know and as I intend to relate them, were otherwise, and it is

[39] *Vita Mosis*, I. 28.
[40] *De Poster. Caini*, 5.
[41] *Enneads*, VI. 9, 11, 8–22.
[42] *Ibid.*, IV. 3, 9, 23–29.
[43] *Ibid.*, V. 3, 17, 27–37.
[44] *Ibid.*, IV. 3, 9, 23–26.
[45] *Ibid.*, II. 9, 12, 31; I. 6, 9, 22–24; see M. de Corte, " Plotin et la nuit de l'esprit," *Etudes Carmélitaines*, II (1938) , 102–15.

Gregory of Nyssa, whom Milton was reading before he wrote *An Apology*, who was the precursor of the Areopagite and who brought this doctrine into the fold of the Church. Gregory invented the poignant oxymoron "bright darkness" (λαμπρός γνόφος),[46] a trope that haunts the rhetoric of mystics ever afterward. In his *Life of Moses* he is troubled by the god who first showed himself in light and then in a dark shroud. He sought and found a solution for this strangeness. The Logos is first seen as light, but as one ascends, it becomes dark because one realizes that it surpasses ordinary knowledge and is separated from mortal comprehension by the *tenebrae*.[47] This is why Moses first saw God as light. Becoming more perfect in understanding by putting aside false knowledge of the divine, he passed from the primary light of the Logos, which dissipates impiety, into the divine dark. In this night, his mind, rejecting "the simple aspects of things," was fixed in a stasis of contemplation so that here he saw the true light where God is.[48] In this way Gregory wrote out the Christian explanations of the dark experience which the person who called himself Dionysius would some centuries later make an intrinsic part of Christian knowledge.

The light metaphysic of the Pseudo-Dionysius also owes much to Origen's doctrine of the double vision obtained through the eyes of the sense and the eyes of the mind. In order that the external eyes of men may be blinded, Origen writes, and that the inner eyes may see, Christ endured the humility of incarnation. By this descent, he, who healed the blind by miracle, blinded our external eyes so that he could cure our inner sight.[49] The Pseudo-Dionysius begins his *Mystical Theology* with the request that he may be allowed to ascend to those oracles where

[46] *In Cantica Canticorum, PG*, XLIV, 1000–1001. It should be noted that Tertullian prior to his polemic against Montanism describes an "obumbratio mentis" as a preface to divine knowledge; see *Ad Marcion, PL*, II, 413, and *De Anima*, ed. Waszink (Amsterdam, 1947), p. 62 and notes. Ambrose considers the *tenebrae* as a requirement of the prophetic state: *De Abraham, PL*, XIV, 484.

[47] *Op. cit., PG*, XLIV, 376–77.

[48] *In Cantica, ibid.*, 1001.

[49] *Contra Celsum, PG*, XI, 1476.

the mysteries of theology are seen in a darkness brighter than light.[50] He yearns to enter the "divine darkness" ($\theta\epsilon\iota o\varsigma$ $\gamma\nu\acute{o}\varphi o\varsigma$),[51] where the human handicap of seeing and being seen is removed and all forms of external perception are blinded in the sacred darkness that is inaccessible light.[52] For him the *tenebrae* is a $\dot{\alpha}\gamma\nu\omega\sigma\acute{\iota}\alpha$; and when the searcher has arrived at its limits, which are complete negation, he will see at last without veils.[53] The Pseudo-Dionysius supports this doctrine with the example of Moses, who penetrated into "the cloud of unknowing" by closing his human eyes to all the vanities of mortal knowledge.[54] Moses, it is true, did not see God's face but only the divine place;[55] nonetheless, his intellectual eyes, like those of the supercelestial Intelligences and Seraphim,[56] were cleansed of the "mass of obscurity."[57]

After the tenth century the vogue of the Pseudo-Dionysius and his doctrine was enormous. Hilduin, John Scot, Hincmar, Radebert, John of Salisbury, Sarrazin, Hugo of St. Victor, Albert the Great, and St. Thomas found spiritual fascination in his writings.[58] The excitement of the Middle Ages was shared by the members of the Florentine Academy, by Ficino, who translated the Areopagite and wrote his own *De Lumine*, and by Pico della Mirandola, who discovered in the Pseudo-Dionysius a fellow exotic. But the light metaphysic of this fifth-century Greek was particularly illuminating to those who followed the upward mystic road, to John of the Cross, Ruusbroec, Tauler, and Suso, all of whom walked the way marked out by Richard

[50] *Op. cit., PG*, III, 997.

[51] *Ibid.*, 1000.

[52] *Epistolae, ibid.*, 1073.

[53] *T.M., ibid.*, 1000–1001.

[54] *Ibid.*, 1001.

[55] *Ibid.*, 1000.

[56] *De Coelesti Hierarchia, ibid.*, 205.

[57] *De Divinis Nominibus, ibid.*, 700–701; see H. C. Peuch, "La Ténèbre mystique chez le Pseudo-Denys," *Etudes Carmélitaines*, II (1938), 33–53.

[58] P. G. Théry, "Denys au moyen age," *Etudes Carmélitaines*, II (1938), 68–74.

of St. Victor [59] and St. Bonaventura. The manuals of the latter saint are rubricated with the paradoxical notion that to see one must become blind: " Excaecatio est summa illuminatio." One must search, says Bonaventura, for the night of light, but only those who have found it know what it is.

Jacob's ladder is placed on these three levels, the top reaching Heaven and so is Solomon's throne where sits the king wise and in peace, lovable as the most precious husband and most desirable. Upon him the angels desire to look and the love of holy souls yearns for him just as the stag seeks fountains of water. Hither in the manner of fire, our spirit is made skillful by a most fervent desire for the ascent but is carried by a wise ignorance beyond itself into darkness and delight so that it not only says with the bride: "We will run after thee to the odor of thy ointments," but also sings with the prophet: "and night shall be my light in my pleasure." What this nocturnal and delightful illumination is no one knows unless he tries it, and unless grace is given divinely no one tries it; and no one is given it unless he trains himself for it.[60]

The same mode of expression is found in Dante, who like Virgil and Milton descended into Hell, who went into the dark in order to see the light. The poetic allegory comes at the beginning when Dante leaves the forest of this world and having endured the night with piety prepares to enter the dark downward path so that he may ascend to the triple circle of final illumination.

> Ma poi ch'io fui al piè d'un colle giunto,
> Là dove terminava quella valle
> Che m'avea di paura il cor compunto,
> Guardai in alto, e vidi le sue spalle
> Vestite già de' raggi del pianeta
> Che mena dritto altrui per ogni calle.
> Allor fu la paura un poco queta
> Che nel lago del cor m'era durata
> La notte ch' io passai con tanta pièta (I. 13–21) .

[59] *Benjamin Minor, PL,* CXCVI, 52.
[60] *Breviloquium, Opera Omnia* (Florence, 1891) , V, 260.

Milton's poetic realization of the themes of descent and ascent, of the necessity of entering the dark in order to see the light, of the descent of light itself so that men may see, and of the inner eye that knows only when the exterior sight is gone, is constantly before us as we read him. These themes were carried to exorbitant excess by the mystics, but we must remember that in spite of the emphasis given them by this nervous faith they have a simple Christian provenience. It is in the plain sense, which seems nowadays to be extravagant, that Milton puts them to use. The descent of humility comes before us as early as the " Nativity Ode " when we are told how the Son of God forsook the " Courts of everlasting Day " to choose " with us a darksome House of mortal Clay." The same theme comes forward again when Christ is assured that he will not degrade his nature " by descending " to assume that of man. " Therefore thy Humiliation shall exalt / With thee thy Manhood also to this Throne " (*PL*, III. 303–14). On the human level the poet seeking perfection rises from the day of " L'Allegro " and enters the night, " the high lonely Tow'r," of " Il Penseroso." Thus he, too, enters the dark, as Moses did, in order to reach the dawn and the " Prophetic strain." As Milton leaves the light of the first poem that reveals only the " aspects of things," Orpheus lifts his head, but in the night of the second he hears the singing of both Orpheus and his son Musaeus. It is in darkness, too, that fallen Adam descends so that the day of fleshly surrender be followed by the night of remorse and humility; through this course, the father of men ascends to God, first, in prayer and, then, in vision.

The theme of the inner eyes, so comforting to the blind man, makes its appearance as early as the *Second Defence*,[61] where Milton compares his blindness with his opponent's spiritual dark: " mine keeps from my view only the colored surfaces of things, while it leaves me at liberty to contemplate the beauty and stability of virtue and truth." *Samson Agonistes*, if it is the last work, almost depends on this idea. At the bottom of despair

---

[61] *Op. cit.*, VIII, 71.

Samson, " a moving grave," doubts that " light is in the Soul "
(92) and sees only " double darkness nigh at hand " (593).
But Samson's night becomes day when in the complete negation of himself he yields humbly to the " rousing motions in
me " (1382) ; then the Semichorus can sing:

> But he though blind of sight,
> Despis'd and thought extinguish'd quite,
> With inward eyes illuminated
> His fiery virtue rous'd
> From under ashes into sudden flame (1687–91).

We must turn, however, to *Paradise Lost*, and especially to two
of its invocations, to find all of this in flower.

The epic opens with the great address recalling Moses' ascent
from the low vale to the summit of Sinai to enter the clouded
light that awaits him. The experience of " that Shepherd, who
first taught the chosen Seed " reminds Milton of the brook of
Siloa which flowed into Siloam's pool, " fast by the Oracle of
God," where Christ healed the blind man, curing at once both
the inward and the exterior eyes. The types of both Old and
New Testament are then personally read as the poet prays for
the ascent toward light. " What in me is dark / Illumine, what
is low raise and support; / That to the highth of this great
Argument...." Prayer is itself the humble act, preface to
Milton's descent into the dark underground of Satan's province.

It is possible that Milton begins in Hell because he who met
Casella " in the milder shades of Purgatory " began there. There
is, however, a difference between the two poets and their pur-
poses. Dante enters Hell (although the allegorical process of
conversion and Christian education is a reader's requirement)
because the literal demanded it. Milton's descent is an artistic
voluntary. In a moral sense Dante descends that he may ascend;
he enters the dark to find the light. In doing so he takes Milton
by the hand, but the reason is doctrinal rather than poetic. Having explored the dark bottom of pride, Milton rises toward the
light. The preface to Book III recounts this ascension:

> Thee I revisit now with bolder wing,
> Escap't the *Stygian* Pool, though long detained
> In that obscure sojourn, while in my flight
> Through utter and through middle darkness borne
> With other notes than to th'*Orphean* Lyre
> I sung of *Chaos* and *Eternal Night*,
> Taught by the heav'nly Muse to venture down
> The dark descent, and up to reascend,
> Though hard and rare (III. 13–21) .

Milton, like Moses, sees the " Holy Light," but like the great type of the Redeemer he must descend to his " Native Element." Light, however, is given the inner eye, and, like Vaughan's Nicodemus, he can " at mid-night speak with the Sun!" It is more than sixteen hundred years after the typified event; yet the English poet joins himself to the procession, heathen and Christian, of those who acted in the great allegory of faith, who descended to ascend, who entered the darkness to see the light.

INDEX